For

Brother Solomon Ali

And

Brother Yahya Ali

Whom I miss everyday.

i

Are You Still A Slave?

Written by Shahrazad Ali

PRESENTED BY

Sistershahrazadali@yahoo.com

Shahrazad Ali, Author

P.O. Box 17124

Cincinnati, OH 45217

Are You Still A Slave?

© 1994 by Shahrazad Ali

Printed in the United States of America
Published by

Shahrazad Ali

P.O. Box 17124

Cincinnati, OH 45217

Are You Still A Slave?

It's not too popular to admit it,
but we can't seem to forget about slavery.
It hangs on like a tiny thorn
pricking the back of our brains.
God knows we have tried to dismiss it.
But we have failed at forgetting
and at pretending to forget.
Perhaps if we go the other way,
and confront this thing once and for all,
we could conquer those left over memories
that breed fear and confusion among us.
We might just rid ourselves
of this inherited mental trauma,
and finally reach that elusive peace
that we all pray for,
called FREEDOM.

CONTENTS

MENTAL PREPARATION
FOR TAKING TEST

Many of us feel a bit reluctant about being selected as needy candidates to take a test titled, "ARE YOU STILL A SLAVE?" Understandably so. The topic of slavery has been by all accounts debated, discussed, written about and politically beaten to death. The seemingly perpetual uptightness caused by our ancestral slave history has already been analyzed a zillion times and been correctly associated with our lack of family values, disunity, unemployment, education, drug and alcohol abuse, premarital sex and multiple other psychologically damaging circumstances of our life. So I agree. There is no further need to keep harping on the worn-out topic of slavery, but there is a definite need to delve deeper into the occurences and incidents that were an integral part of the day to day slave life in order to trace the exact root of many of our problems. We cannot hope to solve our problems until we accurately itemize and dissect the routine daily events that existed during slavery which have a prolonged effect on our personalities. We cannot change our attitudes, habits and ideas until we trace the exact moment, instruction or situation that made such an impact on our development that we continue to be haunted by these destructive tendencies today. Among the myriad of reactions from the brutal slave ancestry that we share, the main question becomes why have certain behaviors remained with us to this very day? Yes, many of us believe or think that slavery happened so long ago, and is so far removed from our contemporary circumstances, that it is impossible for such a buried past to have actual influence on us today. Not so. Psychologists and psychiatrists claim that indeed the opposite is true. We are all unconsciously and subconsciously plagued with repressed past memories which repeatedly control our destiny, and unless resolved, they will continue to be genetically transmitted from one generation to the other. Such is the case of we African-American Blacks. The therapeutic approach of this test provides us with new options of hope and recovery; unlike our past attempts to convince the white power structure that racism does indeed exist, and continues to cause us barriers on social and economic endeavor.

We certainly should realize by now that we are unable to change the system under which we find ourselves living. However, the one remaining portion of our misfortune that we can change is ourselves. While we cannot experientially feel all the physical abuse our ancestors suffered during slavery, we can use this opportunity to examine the happenings of slavery and then make a conscious effort to correct those negative images. By tracing the overt and covert, including subliminal messages transmitted to our ancestors during slavery, we will be able to eliminate those ideas from our brain which we unknowingly still adhere to today.

In other words, we know the cause of our problems, and we know what the problems are, but we do not know how to break the cycle. How to stop having the same problems without government aid or advice. Since none of us want or choose to be a slave, once we isolate the many ways we are still following the guidelines of slavery – which were designed to destroy us; perhaps we will commence to behave and think differently. The ideas drilled into our ancestors have turned out to be more detrimental to our recovery than the racism we encounter now. There is a direct connection between what the slavemaster told us about ourselves and what we think about ourselves right now. The slavemasters were evil in their thinking and they made untrue accusations about us to crush our self-worth and unity as a people. In effect, they lied, and we are living as if what they said was the truth. That belief in itself is what creates the alleged self-fulfilling prophecy we are leaning toward. How to break the mold of our discontent continues to be our most overwhelming challenge. Neither religion nor education have prompted us to change how we behave, what we do or how we act. But if we are able to clearly understand that the bulk of the ideas we have, which we claim as our own, are actually rooted in the inherited mental trauma of slavery; we are bound to make a change . . . since the absolutely very last thing we want to be – is a slave. Being forced to live in a society under racist restraints, yet being required (demanded) to achieve, work and thrive as if everything is normal, has taken a heavy emotional toll on our men, women and children. Each generation of us born since slavery has carried the weight of anger and self-hatred super-glued to our backs with very little let-up. We have been rendered nearly incapable of facing the never ending stumbling blocks placed in our way. While we have made marginal advances socially, educationally and financially, many of the forces that hold us back are not external, many are internal – mental. Hidden away, presumably forgotten, nesting in our brain. Some of us

3

will be surprised to learn that our mentality has not really changed very much at all. Albeit today we have more physical freedom choices, we are still very much emotionally connected to our past. This test is designed to help us make correlations in our life between then and now, and to discover the longevity of our obedience to the rules governing our people during slavery. Rules that were designed to erode our will to live a free productive life. Prior to this test we have focused on our anger as the pivotal point of our distasteful memories about slavery. But brutality was only one form of mistreatment, brainwashing was the psychological process that continues to keep us emotionally fenced in and unable to break free of bondage.

Thus we now have a test to determine, "Are You Still A Slave?" By evaluating the root of your ideas you will arrive at an answer. This test booklet is your private confidential copy, and you are under no obligation to share your results with anyone.

The purpose of this test is to help you identify personal actions, ideas, and habits which are conceivably connected to unconscious flash-backs and repressed memories inherited from our slave history. Likened to Post-traumatic stress syndrome – delayed. For this test to be helpful and constructive, please answer each question as truthfully as possible to the best of your ability. If you lie, you will void the effectiveness of this study, and you will be tricking and robbing yourself of an opportunity to live a peaceful, productive and less-frustrated life. This test is to build you up, not tear you down.

Another purpose of this test is to isolate similar ideas and attitudes which contribute to survival. Since none of us are immune to the psychological damage caused by slavery and the subsequent racism from that event, it behooves us to try to find out why some of us have adapted while great numbers of us have not. Some of the methods already being used to recover will be discussed in the back of this book. Hopefully those who score themselves "FREE" will be able to offer and share recovery techniques with other Black people who are recognizably still a slave – but don't know it. This is the test of our life.

The answers are detailed and explicit in definition, and designed to provoke further self-study and evaluation. Optimistically, your score will indicate that you are "FREE," or on your way to freedom.

However, if your test indicates that you are still a slave, do not become discouraged, because your grade is merely a reflection of your current condition, and does not predict your future potential for recovery. So be honest. And lastly, this test is not to teach or remind you to hate white people, because they are no longer our slavemasters; instead, it is to help you understand your own condition and change it.

NOTE: TURN EACH PAGE ONE AT A TIME
       DO NOT ATTEMPT TO FLIP BACK
        AND FORTH
       Your Personal Score Sheet is at the end of this
       test. Interpretation of your grade is at the end
       of the answer section.
       Take as long as you need.

YOU MAY BEGIN.

TEST OBJECTIVE: To determine if you are plagued
with slavery flashbacks linked
to Post-traumatic Stress, and to
trace the root of your ideas
down to the source.

True means Yes/False means No

1) Our politicians throughout   TRUE   FALSE ✓
   the years have worked hard
   to represent our needs and
   must have our votes to
   continue their progress.

2) It is important to know where   TRUE   FALSE ✓
   I come from, but at this time I
   am better off here, where I am.

3) It is okay to laugh when a   TRUE   FALSE ✓
   Caucasian tells me a joke,
   as long as it is not racially
   offensive in nature.

4) I think it's a good idea when   TRUE ✓ FALSE
   traveling in or out of town to
   always have my I.D. handy
   in case I get a ticket or have
   an accident.

5) The Black church and Black   TRUE   FALSE ✓
   preachers remind us to pray
   for family values, unity and
   spiritual guidance.

6) Telling a lie is not right, but
   since we have been lied to,
   sometimes I have to adjust
   the truth to get something I
   want or to keep the peace.   TRUE   FALSE

7) Native Americans (Indians)
   and us share a common
   history since we were both
   victimized in the same ways
   by the Europeans.   TRUE   FALSE

8) No matter how I feel about
   the police, they are necessary
   to maintain order and protect
   our citizens.   TRUE   FALSE

9) When talking to a white person
   it is best that I keep my
   opinions to myself and not
   let them know what's really
   on my mind.   TRUE   FALSE

10) Black men and women are
    responsible enough to own
    guns if they are not selling
    drugs or robbing banks,
    because having a weapon
    provides security.   TRUE   FALSE

11) Funerals are very important
    in our culture and we attend
    to pay our respects to the
    dead and comfort the family.   TRUE   FALSE

12) As I mature sometimes I suffer   TRUE   FALSE
from various aches and pains
which seem to start and stop
on their own as a natural part
of aging.

13) I think it is a good idea to   TRUE   FALSE
appeal to the government
for reparations to compensate
us for lost wages during
slavery.

14) Although I feel badly about   TRUE   FALSE
it, there are times when I
want to report certain
criminal activities going on
in my neighborhood to the
authorities.

15) A lot has been said about   TRUE   FALSE
sports and games of chance,
but they are really just good
entertainment and safe
recreation.

16) The new wave of Black   TRUE   FALSE
comedians on T.V. are a bit
risque but very funny, and
provide exposure for new talent.

17) Dancing is one of the happiest   TRUE   FALSE
traditions we retained from
our culture and is a symbol of
our freedom and creativity.

18) Sometimes in my relationships   TRUE   FALSE
    I have a problem showing
    nonsexual affection to my
    mate because I am so busy I
    often don't have time to hug
    or embrace my loved ones.

19) It's not that I'm lazy and   TRUE   FALSE
    don't want to work, it's just
    that I feel so unmotivated
    because of lack of skills and
    low paying jobs.

20) Some of our mothers are   TRUE   FALSE
    over-protective and try to
    keep their children with
    them for as long as they
    can so they can feel needed.

21) Even if I give up eating pork,   TRUE   FALSE
    I still enjoy greens & corn-
    bread, candy yams, grits and
    red beans & rice – and
    every once in a while I have
    to have me some of these
    foods – in moderation.

22) Sometimes no matter what I   TRUE   FALSE
    eat or drink I suffer with
    bouts of constipation. As I
    mature I have to be careful
    about what I eat so I can
    keep my bowels open.

23) I hate to walk barefoot, even   TRUE   FALSE
    if it's on carpet. I have to
    have something on my feet
    almost all the time for
    sanitary purposes.

24) Reading to our children and   TRUE   FALSE
    buying them books for
    knowledge and entertainment
    is a very good idea, and we
    should make sure they have
    all kinds of literature to
    keep them interested.

25) It is unfortunate when Black   TRUE   FALSE
    men or boys stand around and
    hold their penis. It is an
    offensive habit and many of
    them do it to be vulgar,
    provocative or rebellious.

26) When I was a child my   TRUE   FALSE
    neighbors or any other adult
    in the community could spank
    me if I was doing something
    wrong, then tell my parents
    and sometimes they would
    whip me again, and it helped
    me become a better person.

27) Although we are not a mono-   TRUE   FALSE
    lithic people, we are all Black,
    and we will eventually come
    together in unity because our
    needs are the same.

28) I think women should work
    outside the home as long as
    they have good, safe and
    affordable day care for their
    children.   TRUE FALSE

29) As long as a man takes care
    of his home obligations,
    there's nothing wrong with
    him going out a lot.   TRUE FALSE

30) I think Black men blow too
    much money on clothes,
    jewelry and cars, but as long
    as they properly provide for
    their families, they should
    have the little extras that
    make them happy.   TRUE FALSE

31) Having "Family Reunions"
    was one of the first new
    traditions our slave
    ancestors established to
    honor the family unit.   TRUE FALSE

32) Hypertension, or high-blood
    pressure is a medical
    problem that Blacks are
    genetically predisposed to
    have, no matter how well we
    take care of ourself.   TRUE FALSE

33) I like highly seasoned foods,
    in fact, salt and hot sauce are
    my favorite spices.   TRUE FALSE

34) Most of our men are frightened   TRUE   FALSE
    and antagonistic about the
    responsibilities of marriage
    and fatherhood.

35) Blacks tend to be more prone   TRUE   FALSE
    to pulmonary heart problems
    and respiratory diseases of
    breathing moreso than whites.

36) It may not be discussed as much   TRUE   FALSE
    anymore, but I still think some
    Black mothers prefer their
    daughters to marry a light-
    skinned African-American or
    even a white man.

37) Unfortunately, some of us are   TRUE   FALSE
    back-stabbers, we sneak
    behind each other and do
    negative things, and care
    little about loyalty if the
    price or benefit of disloyalty
    is worth it.

38) Although camping is not   TRUE   FALSE
    necessarily my idea of fun,
    I do like to attend outdoor
    religious services when
    the weather is really hot.

39) Work is for weekdays, but   TRUE   FALSE
    the weekend, especially
    Saturday night, is for relaxing
    or party-time.

40) When working for white
companies' Black supervisors
(bosses) tend to be more
strict on other Black
employees than a white
person holding a similar
management position.   TRUE   FALSE

41) We should not reject the
European style marriage
ceremony just because we
like more cultural rituals
at our weddings.   TRUE   FALSE

42) Riots and social upheavals
are terrible but they are a
political option we use to
express rebellions and let
off a little steam.   TRUE   FALSE

43) Black churches are now
becoming more racially
mixed (multicultural) not
because whites want to
integrate but because they
like our joyful singing,
music and energetic services.   TRUE   FALSE

44) It is okay if my children go out
and tell others what I talk
about at home, and I should not
reprimand or chastise them for
repeating publicly what I say
in private.   TRUE   FALSE

45) True, we are up from slavery,   TRUE   FALSE
    free and have more rights
    than ever before, but we must
    remember that we are still
    hostages.

46) Sometimes when I am in a   TRUE   FALSE
    small room, crowded elevator
    or large group of people I get
    uncomfortable and start to
    feel suffocated.

47) Even when we complete college,   TRUE   FALSE
    or get skilled training in a
    specific field to become
    successful, it still seems like
    something is missing.

48) Melanin, the Black chemical   TRUE   FALSE
    in our skin, is said to contain
    the entire history of man. We
    have the most lingering memories
    because our race has more
    Melanin than all the others.

49) I am not ready or willing to let   TRUE   FALSE
    go of our negative past and look
    with hope to the future, because
    I don't see things getting any better.

50) Even the most militant among   TRUE   FALSE
    us have to admit that all white
    people are not alike. Despite the
    fact they share the same nature,
    some of them express it differently.

FREEDOM I.Q. SCORE SHEET

1) Each question is worth 2 points. The top possible score is 100.

2) The correct answer for questions
   1-30 is "FALSE"
   How many questions did you mark as "FALSE"?
   Write that number here: _____20_____

3) The correct answer for questions
   31-50 is "TRUE"
   How many questions did you mark as "TRUE"?
   Write that number here: _____6_____

4) Add these two figures together:
   Write total here: _____26_____

5) Multiply the above total times 2

6) Write that number in the box.
   THIS IS YOUR GRADE

   ┌─────────────┐
   │   52   │
   └─────────────┘

7) You may now read the answer section.

8) Interpretation of your numerical grade is at the end of the answer section on page 105.

ANSWER SECTION FREEDOM I.Q. TEST

READ THIS FIRST:

The purpose of the following answers is not to provide you with a fresh set of excuses for our problems, instead they are intended as an explanation from which we may better understand ourselves and stop being slaves.

We have a few grassroots political leaders among us today. Of course, just like back in slavery most of us dislike them, discredit them and insult their efforts at every given opportunity. A few of us delight in getting on white folk's talk shows and speak against them and any of our other so-called leaders. In slavery if a talented slave was given a special post/responsibility or authority – it was always a bogus appointment and the slave could make no move, make no decision or award without the approval of the Master. This is how it is today – we call it "selling out," but it is really only the traditional system used by slaveowners to control the slaves by making them think they are a bigshot of some kind. Today we call this "the illusion of inclusion." Just like in slavery we are taught to criticize and disagree with each other and to be envious and jealous of anything we see each other get.

ANSWERS

> **Q. 1.** Our politicians throughout the years have worked hard to represent our needs and must have our votes to continue their progress.

Answer: FALSE

Every one of our so-called Black leaders has failed at honestly representing our needs or goals for survival. It has been easier to use our supposed leaders against us than in any other race's history. Our leaders are constantly pandering to white politicians and straddling the constituency fence. They are caught up in a dilemma of confused loyalty. In order to be recognized and accepted by their white counterparts they must control their natural aggressiveness, disown their militant views and not make too many demands. They mainly must agree to play by the pre-established political rules made up by whites, give appropriate non-threatening answers when called upon, and publicly renounce other blacks who violate the creed.

Their other problem is one of secret agreement with independent minded blacks who want no part of the white power structure, and angrily tell it like it is, with no adherence to "Robert's Rules of Order." Our leaders are forced to agree with us in private because we are the community he claims to represent and he does not want us to retaliate in the voter's booth or reject him in the media. Our leaders often find themselves trying to defend the very system they already know is corrupt and against our best interests. The slave in leadership positions on the plantation functioned the same way. To protect his own perceived prestige he would side with the slavemaster in order to retain his position of artificial authority. He usually knew whatever the slavemaster was planning for the slaves but he would not reveal this information until given permission from the master. The slave leaders on the plantation were just as fearful of reprisal as are our so-called leaders today. And just as on the plantation, our black leaders today are not a "real" leader until sanctioned and approved of by their white political bedmates (or masters).

Whites have always selected or pre-selected our leaders by crowning them with titles, recognition and media coverage. Once a black leader is ordained and identified by whites, he is evaluated for his penetration potential. If he is deemed to be getting the attention and ear of large numbers of followers or if he is forthright and on target with his demands; he is immediately criticized, ostracized, investigated and kept off the tube and out of the newspapers. His opinions are squashed. On the other hand, if he is an intellectual negro, moderate, malleable and removed from routine contact with poor blacks; he is quickly placed at a podium in the White House and interviewed by every electronic means. If whites support a so-called Black leader you can be sure he is covertly huddling with them, representing their ideas and poses no danger to the status-quo.

The slave leader on the plantation was in a like position. He had to get everything he wanted to do or say approved of by the master first. He was required to make confidential reports to the master and keep him informed of trends or rumors among the slaves or any other strange activity he saw as a potential threat to the master. He would behave just like our leaders today, he would tell the other slaves what he was going to do for them and what they would get in the future. Then after the master turned him down on everything he asked for, he would come back to the slaves with weak excuses for his failure – and a request that they keep the faith and continue to believe in and trust the system because things were going to be better and different the next time around. Of course he always masked his disappointment in front of the master and graciously accepted the master's decision instead of coming up with an alternate independent plan to get what his constituents needed and wanted. The slave leader was constantly getting the door slammed in his face on his ideas, which is the same reception our leaders get today.

> **Q. 2.** It is important to know where I come from, but at this time I am better off here, where I am.

Answer: FALSE

Our ancestors were commanded to denounce their African heritage and to look down on it as savage and comical. The slave master would routinely ask his house-slaves if they wanted to go back to Africa or would they rather stay there with him. Of course, the slave always gave the appropriate answer since he did not want to be struck for admitting he wanted to go back to his homeland. Today Africa is under the influence of the same kind of colonization ideas that founded America.

And no, we do not want to go back to Africa to live today. We are spoiled by the so-called modern conveniences of American domestic life. We continue to have a repugnance to growing our own food and livestock and processing our own natural resources and turning them into what we need and want. It's easier to run to the corner store or shop at the mall. It's entirely possible that we should reject Africa and America as a permanent home. Perhaps we should look elsewhere. The earth is spinning and we're on it. Plus, if we through some stretch of the imagination wound up back in Africa, they would soon expel us from among them because of our laziness and inability to follow or take instructions from another Black person. We consider many life saving tasks as menial labor which insults our ego because our ancestors were forced to do menial labor during slavery and it took on a negative connotation that lingers with us today. And due to our hunger to have a culture we can identify with, we emulate the fabrics, colors, headwear, garb and symbols of Africa. And if we are honest, Africa is alright for a visit, but not as a permanent home. The culture shock would be too great for us to stand.

We can't leave out the masterful beauty of the land nor the magnificent artful creations our ancestors created. But Africa is in hell today. Nearly the whole continent has been disrupted by European-American-Asian interference in their affairs. A global rip-off of Africa's natural resources by the enemy.

Q. 3. It is okay to laugh when a Caucasian tells me a joke, as long as it is not racially offensive in nature.

Answer: FALSE

Slaves were forced to laugh at the masters' jokes during slavery, even if the joke was on them. They were expected to laugh when the master laughed and cry when he cried. They thought sharing in laughter with the master would make him more relaxed in his dealings with them and would promote informal comradship and acceptance. They were forced to laugh even if the joke was about the beating or maiming of another slave or family member. Slaves learned to smile as soon as they saw the master to make him think that they were perpetually happy and pleased to be in his service. A sullen look often earned a swat across the head — so we learned to grin. Early movies depict us as all teeth, laughing and grinning, forever pleasant ready to serve. Big eyes and all. Through the years, whites have maintained this practice of telling us jokes, not necessarily offensive or lewd, just ordinary stories they think are funny. They still think it's a way to test our mood or attitude – so they tell a joke and we pretend that it's funny and laugh so as not to offend them or hurt their feelings. Whenever we do that, we are still reacting like a slave. Whites tend to think that we have an exaggerated ever present sense of humor, and we tend to think that laughing at their jokes is just routine pleasantry. Neither is true. Many a slave reports of sitting up half the night laughing at their master's jokes and then going to bed and crying all night in their pillow from the cruel humiliation of pretended amusement. So we should stop laughing at white people's joke telling because ain't nothing funny between us and them. If you are no longer a slave, stop laughing on cue. Once we stop laughing at their jokes it will eliminate a lot of useless communication between us. All dialogue will be reduced to necessary communication. Serious and void of humor.

Q. 4.   I think it's a good idea when traveling in or out of town to always have my I.D. handy in case I get a ticket or have an accident.

Answer: TRUE and FALSE

True, it is a legal requirement that every citizen residing in America must always have I.D. with them, on their person. It may not be a law on the books, but it is an unwritten requirement of the police that we be able to prove who we are at any given moment. This is an old slavery practice that said a slave could never be out after dark or out of their own neighborhood without a written note from the master describing the location he was permitted to travel and the purpose of the errand. This was called having "papers." We use the term loosely to describe when we are fired or dismissed from a post, or shut out of a relationship – we say "he got his walkin' papers." "Papers" were the permission to leave format designed by the master to keep tabs on loose negroes and to always know their whereabouts. There are so many seemingly innocent but insidious practices that are holdovers from slavery. Procedures have not changed as much as we think.

A southern Act of 1740 said: "If any slave who shall be out of the house or plantation where such slave shall live or shall usually be employed, or without some white person in company with such slave, shall refuse to submit to undergo the examination of <u>any</u> white person, it shall be lawful for any such white person to pursue, apprehend, and moderately correct such slave; and if such slave shall assault and strike such white person, such slave may be lawfully killed."!!! (Brevard's Digest 231) A variation of this rule, including stop, search and seize, is still in effect for every Black man in America, and increasing numbers of Black females also. What makes us all look suspicious to the police is that we are Black (ex-slaves) who might be out up to no good.

Q. 5. The Black church and Black preachers remind us to pray for family values, unity and spiritual guidance.

Answer: FALSE

Our Black preachers are the sole representatives of keeping slavery intact, using the Bible as their method of induction. A 1950's sociologist, E. Franklin Frazier, raised the question as to whether the negro population was "over-churched." Indeed it is.

Preaching the gospel of christianity was the first position/job that the slave master allowed the Black man to have because they viewed it as non-threatening (when taught as they instructed), and as a helpmate to them in convincing slaves to accept bad treatment as only a temporary condition. One slave master in North Carolina reportedly said, "the Christian religion sustains rather than threatens slavery, the 'gospel is the mightiest safeguard' because it governs in secret as well as in public, by cultivating a conscience connected to the lord." The slave masters believed that slaves who were the most intimately acquainted with the Bible, best understands the relationship between master and slave and are the most contented with it. The slave preacher and his establishment of church services provided the original "soap-box" opportunity for Black men to get special attention, rule others via religious doctrine, set political tones in the community, and get special favors from both whites and blacks. The post carried broad status on and off the plantation, not only confined to spiritual matters. They always got first choice of the women and free meals any day of the week and overnight lodging if necessary. It was considered an honor to have the preacher visit you. It still is in most of our communities, and the preacher still gets the same benefits as he got in slavery plus more.

Preaching (setting up a church) continues to be a business requiring the least amount of up-front capital, equipment or customers. The Black pulpit continues to retain a vice-like grip on the emotions and minds of countless Blacks who show up weekly for a new dose of "pie-in-the-sky" sedation.

We continue to believe that the slavemaster lied to us about everything but God, while we continue to use the exact same book (the Holy Bible) that they originally gave to us after we had been enslaved for almost 100 years. New interpretations not withstanding, the text, the theme and the promises are exactly the same. And consequently, so are we.

Most preachers are leader wannabes void of a platform so they use religion to attract an audience over which they expound on their views. There are many Black preachers who are doing good work in their communities and the church provides them with an institution from which to work, but they are "saving" our people from the streets, and immediately placing them in classes to teach them slavery. They often elicit their help in going back into the streets to round up more converts who will also be indoctrinated with the techniques and ideas of slavery. Their work is devalued because they attract black people by using the scriptures the slavemasters used to dominate us.

Q. 6. Telling us a lie is not right, but since we have been lied to, sometimes I have to adjust the truth to get something I want or to keep the peace.

Answer: FALSE

As we all know by now, us lying to each other remains a problem of monumental proportion. We have learned to justify lying as a way to survive. We have categorized lies into compartments such as lying to keep from hurting someone, lying to make someone feel good, lying to get credit, lying to get a job, lying to avoid punishment, lying to make an impression and lying to hide the truth about ourselves. We don't realize that every time we tell a lie we complicate our lives because we have to commit that lie to our permanent memory and be ever ready to recite it exactly as we told it the first time. This adds stress. We justify lying to whites as excusable because we know of many incidents where they have lied to us. But lying is the way out for a coward. Speaking the truth regardless to whom or what, takes great courage – of which most of us don't have at the moment.

During slavery the slave was taught that his word had absolutely no value, and that his promises and agreeing contained no binding force legally. This reduced the value of telling the truth in the slave since he was not apt to be believed one way or the other. Slaves also learned to lie to save their life by giving the master whatever answer he wanted to hear for reassurance that the slaves were happy. The slaves also lied to each other because they grew to distrust each other based on their individual desperation. Any slave might go and report something to the master to get the slave in trouble and win some sort of favor or browny points for future use. So lying was first cultivated in slavery and we have developed it into a high science. Justified and proven valid by long lists of personal rewards we gained from the act.

No wonder we tell so many lies we resorted to lying back in slavery in order to survive. Lying is an old habit cultivated to trick the slavemaster into letting us live. Unfortunately today we use it in our personal relationships and on the job and with our friends in order to keep the peace, brag or get ahead. Lying is not a good idea and we get caught sooner or later.

Q. 7. Native Americans (Indians) and us share a common history since we were both victimized in the same ways by the Europeans.

Answer: FALSE

The American Indians were here when we arrived. The Europeans had tried capturing and using the Indians for labor but they proved not to be physically strong enough, and since they were on their home turf they were familiar with the terrain and easily escaped leaving no followable trail. Indians were first introduced to Black slavery when the Europeans would give them a negro slave as a gift when they were first trying to trick them out of their land or gain access to hunting grounds. Every kind of trick was tried usually with success. They next hired the Indians to track down runaway slaves. They routinely offered them gifts for the capture of a Black slave such as: watches, coats, muskets, blankets, hatchets or gun flints. Some runaway slaves managed to hook up with the Indians and disappear into the mountains. Indians who were studying the whiteman's use of blacks as slaves would occasionally purchase a black slave so they too could own a worker who they did not have to pay. The Cherokee Indians were notorious for approving of Black slavery – especially after they becamse scattered as the whiteman pressed westward, and they lost their base communities and had to operate individual farms isolated from their tribes. The black slaves relieved the Cherokee women of the backbreaking household tasks they were responsible for. The slaves performed tanning, weaving and making pottery. Slaves had a better life with the Indians than they had with the whites according to historians.

Q. 8.   No matter how I feel about the police, they are necessary to maintain order and protect our citizens.

Answer: FALSE

We have no historical proof that the laws of the U.S.A. have ever maintained order for us or protected us from abuse. We have the same complaints about the legal system today as our ancestors had during slavery. We have never had equal protection under the law. The slaves charged that they were punished with more severity for similar crimes committed by whites who were only fined or exonerated. The American slave code has always provided that the enactment of penal laws is for the protection and security of those who make the laws. That posture obviously eliminated the slaves from any and all considerations concerning justice since they were not permitted to have any vote or voice in legal or political matters.

The first laws used in reference to slaves were originally taken from "Roman civil law" and was using in the slave states because they contained the principle of that "peculiar institution."

We blacks have never made any laws in America. In slavery our ancestors were under the control of the law although unprotected by the same law. After slavery our ancestors charged the courts with unequal justice, no jury of their peers, long sentences for minor infractions, penal abuse, police brutality, cruel and unusual punishment and taxation without representation. These same complaints are lodged every day in every Black community across America. We are still subjected to laws we had no input in making and laws that often work against us in particular.

The "American Slave Code" is still in effect concerning Blacks and the law. Some think that new laws are made to legally violate us but they are not new laws, just old laws which have remained on the books in more sophisticated language.

Q. 9. When talking to a white person it is best that I keep my opinions to myself and not let them know what's really on my mind.

Answer: FALSE

This habit goes back to practicing agreeable dishonesty manifested in being the "happy negro." Always doing fine, "yassir masta, I's doin' good." Just as mentioned in ANSWER #3, trying to always appear as if all is well is a holdover from our slave history when we were forced to make false representations to secure our wellbeing. It was also used to keep the slave master unaware of our true feelings. It was a way to have a tiny bit of leverage. However, we tend to make complaints about whites behind their backs or with large groups of people in discussion, but when faced one on one, something happens and we tend to clam up and rather talk about the weather or any other unimportant topic. It was fear that held us back in slavery from telling whites how we really felt, make a new step in rejecting slave behavior and speak up and speak out, make comments on any subject you choose. Rid yourself of feelings of shame or inadequacy, tell them whatever you are compelled to admit. This is not an antagonistic suggestion. It is a suggestion to be more open with the people who possibly represent your greatest emotional threat. If, on the other hand, you are more comfortable presenting them with an artificial personality, image and tone of voice; you must seriously consider psychotherapy to end the slavery flash-backs you are having that prevent you from "being yourself" in the presence of whites. Your fear has gotten out of hand. Also, if you are working on a job which requires you to maintain the facade of being "the happy negro," you should change, or remove yourself from an environment that expects you to continue to react like a slave.

> **Q. 10.** Black men and women are responsible enough to own guns if they are not selling drugs or robbing banks, because having a weapon provides security.

Answer: FALSE

After slavery was legally abolished on paper, thousands of Black men, former slaves, rushed to purchase and own weapons/guns which were now permissible for them to have. All slaves who were able began to partake of all sorts of "goodies" previously withheld from them. The newly found freedom created what historians call "freedom panic" and since there were no systems in place to make the emotional shift from slavery to freedom a smooth transition, the slaves became over-hyped and recklessly excited. This excitement coupled with their new access to guns and rifles stirred up new power in them and propelled formerly docile and controlled rage into Black trigger fingers. When they got guns they didn't rush out and start shooting their ex-masters, instead, they pointed their guns at the exact image of who they had been taught for four centuries to hate. Many of them wounded or killed themselves because the guns were faulty. There are no records throughout intensive investigation about slavery where a Black man was charged with shooting a white man and living to go to trial about it. And as today, when a Black man shoots another Black man, the penalty is much less than if he shot a white man. Blacks shooting and killing blacks today is no different than the reaction our slave ancestors had when they acquired guns during slavery. And the slaves obtained guns after slavery from the same source we are getting them from now, and this same source knows full well what Blacks have been emotionally programmed to do when they get their hands on a weapon.

We are still not emotionally stable enough to own or carry guns.

Q. 11. Funerals are very important in our culture and we attend to pay our respects to the dead and comfort the family.

Answer: FALSE

The way that we handle funerals (death) must be put into perspective. First we view the body in the funeral home then file past it in a single line at the funeral. Even if the casket is closed during the funeral, it is currently our custom to file past the casket and look at the burial box of the deceased as a way of showing respect for the dead. Our funerals are one of the most heart wrenching often hysterical events most of us have ever known. The grief is milked to a fever pitch by long eulogies, sad songs and group wailing.

This is not the way death was handled prior to slavery, and it used to be a solemn dignified affair, with mostly only members attending. Our current system of filing past the dead, gazing into the face of the dead person, and sometimes even kissing the corpse is a process derived from slavery.

During the long and arduous trip to the Americas on slave ships, whenever there was a particularly rebellious slave aboard, or a slave who openly fought against the ship's crew, that slave was killed in a way to set an example and put fear in the other slaves. The slave was usually hung up by the wrist tied with a rope or leather strap. They were lashed/beaten for two or three days prolonging death to the last moment. After that, the slave was decapitated, his or her body was thrown overboard to be devoured by sharks or other killer fish. The head of the slave was displayed in a prominent spot on the ship and for several days afterward the remaining slaves were forced to walk past the head and kiss it. Africans believed that the head of a dead person must stay intact after death, as this was part of certain religious beliefs on the dark continent. Being forced to view and kiss the dead head of a comrade caused intense emotional and mental anguish among the Black men, women and children on the slave ships. Instead of death remaining a natural part of the progress of life, it was turned into a long and drawn out terrifying event. As it is today.

A recent example of this technique is how in Ferguson, MO when the St. Louis Police Department left Michael Brown's bullet ridden bloody body lying in the street all day to send a message to the local citizens. No doubt many adults and children were visually traumatized by this open disregard for Black life and disrespect of the victim's parents and family.

Q. 12. As I mature sometimes I suffer from various aches and pains which seem to start and stop on their own as a natural part of aging.

Answer: FALSE

Psychologists have identified a condition they call "body memories" and unfortunately we are victims of this maladjustment also. Deep within our psyche, perhaps hidden in our fallopian tubes and buried within our sperm there rests these ancient "body memories" consisting of frequent complaints of psychosomatic aches and pains. Psychosomatic means that the pain is real but the source is imaginary. Blacks who suffer from these imaginary aches and pains tend to, after intense physical and medical examinations, accept the aches and pains as part of their lives. Sometimes they settle on believing they have arthritis, neuralgia or muscle spasms of unknown origin. They often take dangerous medications every day, hourly, to control what they believe are actual ailments. The root cause of these "body memories" are from the physical brutality our ancestors endured during slavery. Whippings, beatings, kickings, branding, pinching, shoving, thrashing and punches are some of the types of brutalities suffered. The disease of "body memories" are said to also be experienced by people who lose large amounts of weight, or who had had limbs dismembered but still feel like they are hurting in a hand, leg or arm – which they no longer have attached to their body. "Body memories" if left undiagnosed can be extremely dangerous because of their addictive quality. The aches and pains experienced during "body memories" can cause us to feel limited in our aspirations, and make us think we are unable to achieve because of our perceived physical disabilities. Biofeedback is a good method to employ to rid ourselves of "body memories" and to mentally control the pain and eventually eliminate it altogether.

The brain has many defenses to protect itself, while the physical body only has two; numbness and pain. And our bodies have not forgot.

BODY MEMORIES may take many forms,
such as:

Chest Pain	Vomiting
Dizziness	Stomach ache
Headache	Diarrhea
Fatigue	Constipation
Lump in Throat	Back pain
Amnesia	Joint pain
Nausea	Genital ache

As in all studied cases of abuse, the repressed memories of any incident can be emotionally triggered and brought to the surface by certain objects, odors, surroundings or any exposure to activities or situations that resemble the original trauma. Slave recollections are so frightening and painful that we avoid any activity or symbol that even remotely reminds us of our trauma. Since each of us have an individual blood line connection, the ordinary looking incident in daily life takes on exaggerated importance. Our Post-traumatic Stress Disorder prevents us from summoning the innate coping mechanisms necessary to overcome, so we become suspicious bordering on paranoia. Thus every obstacle encountered will be perceived as a signal of danger.

Then comes "fight or flight," then comes indecision and frustration. We don't know what to do.

Q. 13. I think it is a good idea to appeal to the government for reparations to compensate us for lost wages during slavery.

Answer: FALSE

Many of us believe that the American government owes us an unpaid debt incurred during slavery when our ancestors were forced to provide free labor to help build this great country. We think that as their descendants we have a right to inherit their belated compensation – hopefully in the form of money. This perpetual belief that our oppressors will one day see the light and do the right thing is an unfounded faith in the eventual good of all humanity. Nothing could be further from the truth. Many of our ancestral slave relatives believed that if they worked hard enough, were cooperative and obedient and made the master happy; that one day he would grant them their freedom, not sell their children, and not beat their mates. There are few recorded instances where this actually happened, but the idea was comforting to the slaves and gave them a hope, however mystical, that one day they would get something for their labor. Some families in the south infrequently were awarded with plots of land, given or willed to them by their ex-masters, usually after his death. None of this was done out of feelings of incurred debt. The slave master enjoyed the feeling of being beneficient, thinking that he took good care of his slaves and was their ultimate benefactor. But he reserved the right to make his own decisions about who deserved what and who would get whatever. This is the same predicament we are in today. The government has not, will not, and never will admit that they owe us anything more than what they think they are already giving us. They do not feel duty bound or obligated in any way to pay us back for any wages resulting from our ancestors' labor. To wait on this to happen is a nightmarish pipedream. Just like we think we are up out of slavery, whites believe they, too, are finished being slave masters.

Any payment defined as reparations would mean that the government would be admitting their ancestors did gross wrong to our ancestors, something so obligating that it warranted financial renumeration to the descendants of the people they wronged. It will never happen. It's hard enough getting paid for the work we do now, less known receiving any compensation for some work performed over 400 years ago by deceased relatives. The Slave Laws said in the Civil Code of Ethics, Art. 35 clearly states, "A slave can possess nothing nor acquire anything but what must belong to his master." They cannot take by purchase or descent. Slaves have no legal rights in things, real or personal, additionally, 'slaves are incapable of inheriting or transmitting property' (Civil Code, Art. 945). There are laws on the books which directly prohibit slaves from transmitting an inheritance (even though there was none implied in the first place). We waste valuable thinking and planning time wishing and hoping that one day the American government or the United Nations or the ghost of

Christmas past is going to give us the big pay-back for enslaving us.

> **Q. 14.** Although I feel badly about it, there are times when I want to report certain criminal activities going on in my neighborhood to the authorities.

Answer: FALSE

There are recorded in history only three (3) major slave rebellions and all of them were duly foiled by dedicated passive house slaves. There has always been conflict between the house slave and the field slave. The house slaves tended to think that the field slave was a low grade untrained Sambo whose ignorant behavior represented a threat to their cushy better-off position in the master's private quarters. The field slave resented the house slave and was distrustful of the step-in-fechit methods used to get assigned an indoor post. The field slave was somewhat of an embarassment to the house slave. The house slave would periodically visit the field slave quarters and come back and report to the master. The house slave would also make investigations of other house slaves and report on them too. He always wanted the master to think he was on his side and was sincere in his efforts to "do the right thing."

Today we have Blacks who are too timid, too scared and too modern to challenge the illegal activities in their communities, so they sneak and call the white man, or tell the press or write an anonymous letter to the local precinct to report suspicious activities.

It is entirely possible that they are right. Much of what goes on among our people standing around on corners or in alleys is super wrong. There is no argument on those points. But there is something about snitching to the authorities that comes from slaves accustomed to calling in the master for his intervention and authority to settle disputes or problems on the plantation that the slaves could not settle themselves. Slaves were not allowed to make

Today in many urban area police departments nationwide they claim they are working with low budgets and therefore are cutting back on routine neighborhood services. Examples: They no longer come out to record or investigate domestic violence incidents (unless someone is killed), no more interest in routine home burglaries (if no one is hurt), hit and run accidents off the main streets are ignored, etc. They now say that if you are really interested you can go down to the police station and file your own report. But let a cat get caught up in a tree and they send out the entire fire department to rescue the cat out the tree or a dog out a sewer. They have always been more sympathetic to injured animals of any kind than they have been to Black people in America. Back during slavery if a Black was hurt they would call the veterinarian to care for us. This idea that animals are better than we are and deserve more consideration is not new. The judicial system will give a person a longer sentence for injuring an animal than killing a human being, especially if that human being is African-American/Black.

42

> **Q. 15.** A lot has been said about sports and games of chance, but they are really just good entertainment and safe recreation.

Answer: FALSE

Adults did not play sports in Africa as part of their daily routine. Certainly there were community events, competitions, celebrations, initiations and such; but there was no game playing among the men who were most serious about survival and responsibility. The absorption into sports and playing games originated in slavery when our men were forced to perform feats that the master bet on, or to box bare-knuckled nearly to death for the entertainment of the master and his friends. Sometimes games were devised by the slaves themselves to make the time pass faster or for small wagers among themselves. This only took place on Saturday or Sunday because six days out of seven, or sometimes seven out of seven, the slaves had to work the fields and tend their children and shanties.

Sports are used by us today as a diversion, a distraction and a transference of physical aggressiveness. The sounds and movements in sports allow us, especially our men, to be voyeurs of a sort, and allows them to safely release certain repressed feelings of bondage. Our men are attracted to physical competitions because they want to win at something – even if it's a team effort – or even if it is winning by proxy (by selecting the right team as a winner).

Focusing on a ball or other objects allows us to subconsciously make it the focal point of our challenges. Needless to say, too much time is spent idle watching sports, playing games and betting instead of trying to improve our condition. There is not much hope for us to persuade Black men from wasting time with sports, they are addicted to them by now and look forward to the emotional release that sports provide them with. Our Black athletes, despite being paid huge sums of money, still "perform" for and are paid by the same group whom our ancestors performed for during slavery.

Q. 16. The new wave of Black comedians on T.V. are a bit risque but very funny, and provide exposure for new talent.

Answer: FALSE

For many years science and psychology have concluded that self-esteem or self-image plays an integral part in successful human development. Today's onslaught of young Black comedians, male and female, defy all logic regarding self-image and respectful public behavior. The type of gutter language and savage talk that these so-called comedians use is not acceptable by civilized human beings in the seclusion of their own homes, or on national television in front of 20 or 30 million viewers. This show business "craft" is defended because of its publicity value which may lead to future engagements for the comedians. Black comedy allegedly has always been a bit off-color and raunchy. The skits are base and embarrassing to mixed company.

Throughout slavery, as soon as blacks found that the master could be easily entertained or distracted by a little fancy toe-tapping or jolly singing; blacks developed another new skill: that of "acting funny." They performed amusing tricks and hilarious stunts to coerce the master into a happy spirit or less-mean attitude. This knack of "being funny" is one shared by many of us, on and off the stage. Since the master's sense of humor was vastly different from the slave's, they had to go to great extremes to keep him amused and off their case. They saw making him laugh as approval, a source of affection and acceptance. Being funny is a drastic attempt to gain access to the softer side of others by distracting them with laughter. Some of us seem to be born with a natural ability to exaggerate situations and stories so that each explanation comes out funny. Physical animation goes along with this trait and out of this mixture arises another leftover trauma of slavery — one of classic buffoonery. Also called "cutting the fool," or "acting like a fool." We should stop.

> **Q. 17.** Dancing is one of the happiest traditions we retained from our culture and is a symbol of our freedom and creativity.

Answer: FALSE

We have always taken great pride in our apparent inborn talent for dancing. We are able to move fluidly, with or without music, with a nearly instinctive ability to glide from creative to contemporary to erotic to demonstrate our smoothness and agility on the dance floor. Dancing was on the top of the narrow list of cultural expressions the slave master allowed to continue during slavery. Dancing was followed by singing. Our first introduction to dancing for the slave master was on the ships that brought us here. Every morning, in order to keep our joints lubricated, the ship hands forced us to dance – jump up and down on the deck – to the tune of bagpipes, harps, fiddles or drums. Our "dance" was excruciatingly complicated by the heavy iron chains around our ankles and wrists, but nevertheless we were prodded into jumping up and down actually as a sadistic form of exercise.

Certain types of dancing have been identified by many psychoanalysts over the past several decades, to be an outlet for release of negative energy made appealing by the accompaniment of music and finger popping. Dancing, like exercise, tends to rid us of pent up tension. Our particular type of dancing also reveals the nature and mood of our people, especially our youth. This is why the dance movements of our teenagers today are so frenetic and frenzied, and impossible to be duplicated by middle-agers or older adults. They are "acting out" their frustrations to the crass tempos of their music. Young people tend to dance with the most energetic motions because instinctively they see waiting in their peripheral vision the barriers and suffocating pressure of the emptiness of their futures. Their dance is one of panic and hysteria. As we grow older our dance movements seem to become stagnated to one-foot, one at a time, from side to side in a swaying motion; because by that time we have learned to accept our limitations and frailties and no longer feel the urge to demonstrate our internal rage in dancing. We refer to this stage as maturity, when it is really only the stage in which we are finally able to intellectualize our internal animosities and turn them into a distorted settling down. Yes, during our ancestral slave history our people, when allowed, often danced with wild abandon for hours on end. They danced because of giant weariness, huge loneliness and individual helplessness. In Africa dances had meaning, told stories or expressed ideals. Dancing was not just used to move the body to the beat of music. For us it has always been a means of communication.

Even sounds like grunts had a certain meaning. All words influence thoughts, ideas and actions. The tone of a word can set attitudes, happiness or sadness. It has already been proven during wartimes that playing certain words or sounds over and over in a someone's ear can drive them literally crazy. Even a steady drop of water if repeated long and often enough has been known to disrupt the sleep and thinking patterns of humans. So it is ridiculous to think that certain derogatory words and terms repeated at high volume all day and all night have no impact on the behavior of the listener.

Q. 18. Sometimes in my relationships I have a problem showing nonsexual affection to my mate because I am so busy I often don't have time to hug or embrace my loved ones.

Answer: FALSE

Slaves were not allowed to touch, show affection or demonstrate any type of caring relationship to other slaves while in sight of the master or any of his white workers or overseers. Of course they were able to sneak around and spend time with each other, but the master wanted control of selecting all matings and couplings among the slaves. He maintained this unnatural control to assure himself of the slaves inhumanness which required breeding them like other farm animals.

The law covering the showing of affection or attempts to bond said: "A slave cannot even contract matrimony, the association which takes place among slaves, and is <u>called</u> marriage, being properly designated by the word contubernium, a relation which has no sanctity, and to which no civil rights are attached," (Stroud's 'Sketch of the Slave Laws'). "Nor were they the proper objects of cognation or affinity, but quasi-cognation only," (The Elements of Civil Law). The law makers and slave masters could not sanction holy marriage between slaves because the promise of the husband to protect his wife and provide for her were not liberties or opportunities afforded to a slave man.

While there are selected cases where the master permitted a semblance of a real marriage between slaves who professed love for each other, slaves feeling greatly inspired by their love for another

48

slave always managed to figure out how to be together secretly. Eventually the master, who actually liked to refer to himself as a farmer, loosened the reigns on trying to control conjugal affairs among the slaves. He began to realize the economic potential of allowing the slaves to mate on their own decisions – there would be more children to grow into slaves or to sell on the open market. However, the slaves never let go of the idea of "sneaking" around to be with each other. We also see the effect of that idea today in the clandestine infidelities in our relationships.

Q. 19. It's not that I'm lazy and don't want to work, it's just that I feel so unmotivated because of lack of skills and low paying jobs.

Answer: FALSE

The workday of the slave was from sun-up to late nite. The only incentive to work was the sting of the whip or the threat of 30 lashes, since there was no chance for economic advancement. To emotionally compensate for being forced to work with no pay, the slaves had no incentive or motivation to work well, so they did everything possible to stage slow-downs whenever the opportunity arose. They worked as slow as permitted by the glaring overseer in order to do as little as possible in the longest span of time. Work undone or half-done, orders forgotten, lying and thievery set in motion an opinion by the master that slaves were dumb – but these were protests. The master studied the slaves' effectivity during a workday and mathematically calculated that slaves were barely two-thirds as efficient as a free worker who earned regular wages. But the slavemaster made up for the slack time by working the slaves longer or adding more slaves to the job. The work ethics of our people at that time mirror the work ethics of many of us today. Some of us even brag about how we do "as little as possible" just to make the time go by as long as we are on the clock. Some of us hide-out in the bathroom, others take extra-long breaks or lunches, still others have mastered the disguise of "looking busy" when in fact we are not doing anything productive at all. This could be tossed in with "malingering" – fraudulent attempts to obtain undeserved compensation. All of this behavior, referred to as "lazy" by onlookers, is actually a way to retaliate against the boss, owner or supervisor.

Blacks today blame their lack of enthusiasm about work on the same reasons the slaves had for not working 400 years ago. They say the pay is too low, the benefits too few, no recognition or special appreciation, no chance at ownership or title advancement. Same. Same.

> **Q. 20.** Some of our mothers are over-protective and try to keep their children with them for as long as they can so they can feel needed.

Answer: FALSE

Some form of separation anxiety is played out in most Black households when it is time, or when a child decides it is time to break away from the security of the parental abode and establish a nest of its own. No matter how much the child begs, proves or explains their readiness to leave; there is some type of flare-up emotionally riddled on both sides. The parents, especially the mother, tries to hold on a little longer and may even cling to the child. Black mothers tend to have difficulty in releasing a child to the wide wide world of independence. Or so it seems. This type of behavior in our mothers is seen as an attempt to control the child's mobility or unwarranted overprotectiveness.

Separations always created a problem for our slave ancestors – be it based on the forced departure of a loved one sold off, or from danger and apprehension about a mate who decided to make a run, and try to break for freedom. Of course the most painful parting of them all was when the master would sell the child away from the wanting arms of a mother – who would rather die than give up her baby. This condition is symptomatic in our Black women today who may exhibit irrational grief or extreme panic when her child decides to go. We have had so many babies snatched from our breast, wrung from our arms or ripped out our wombs; that every time a child departs from us we re-live that horror. This kind of separation anxiety may drift into deep depression which lasts several weeks until the mother is assured, by her own standards, that the child will survive and that she can reach, touch or see it at will. A more acceptable and contemporary way Black mothers handle this is to claim happiness and relief that a child is finally leaving home, releasing the parent from obligation. This is not our system. Our way is extended family living.

Q. 21. Even if I give up eating pork, I still enjoy greens & cornbread, candy yams, grits and red beans & rice – and every once in a while I have to have me some of these foods – in moderation.

Answer: FALSE

You probably already know that none of these foods are good for you, but we should stop eating them for both health and emotional reasons. During slavery our ancestors existed on a repetitive diet of foods which were of the lowest quality imaginable. From the moment they stepped on the slave ship their first introduction to the plantation diet was beans and rice and yams (sweet potatoes). Sometimes their diet was supplemented with rotted fish which had lain in the sun all day up on deck, or scraps of putrid smelling salted pork. Food was sparse on the slave ships and the Europeans who manned the ships, especially if they did not hold rank, were forced to sustain themselves on the same diet the slaves had. Many times the shipmates would instigate a problem among the slaves when the captain was not around so they would have to kill them and toss their bodies overboard in order to have more food for themselves. Older ship logs from slave ships hint that the European deck hands ate some of the slaves when food became scarce. It was difficult stocking food because there was no refrigeration and above and below deck was scorching hot during the day. Greens, cornmeal bread and the offal organs of the pig were added after the slaves arrived on the plantation. But beans and rice was the very first diet forced on the slaves after they were snatched up out of Africa. Today we call these foods "Soul Food" or down home country cooking and these foods make up the menu in a lot of Black homes and restaurants. Pig tails, pig knuckles, chittlins, fat back, pig feet and ribs are considered prize meals and part of our culture. They are part of our culture, but not a part we need to emulate and keep alive. We must separate our stomachs from these foods which represent paying homage to our bondage and subjugation. Eating these foods was not a form of joy or celebration among our slave ancestors, and neither should it be for us. Give up the slave diet.

> **Q. 22.** Sometimes no matter what I eat or drink I suffer with bouts of constipation. As I mature I have to be careful about what I eat so I can keep my bowels open.

Answer: FALSE

There are medical statistics which say that constipation is a routine health problem for us and taking laxatives to move our bowels is a sort of bogus cultural practice among Blacks and we have been known to prescribe a laxative for a multitude of physical complaints.

Due to the abrupt change in diet that our ancestors were forced to partake of to stay alive on the slave ships, it disrupted their bowel evacuation schedules. The immediate reaction to the new diet was to develop diarrhea, plus, the sickening smells below deck where the slaves were stacked like sardines in a can, caused further bowel problems. The uncomfortable sitting and laying coupled with a new and repulsive diet caused such extreme intestinal reactions that diarrhea, followed by dehydration, often lasted for weeks. The expelled feces were filled with blood and mucus from the poor food and sleeping conditions. The deck hands hated this condition among the slaves and were repulsed by the smell of excrement from possibly a thousand rectums all at once. So the deck hands would flog (beat) the slaves who continued to mess up the wooden deck when they were brought up each day to eat and have exercise, and breathe fresh air. So the slaves tried to suppress this involuntary act and would squeeze their anus so tightly to avoid getting beat and would strain so violently that they caused

54

themselves to have a prolapsed rectum – which they received no medical care for. Many of them refused food to keep from having diarrhea. Those who refused to eat were beaten or had hot coals applied to their lips. Many died from this.

Modern psychologists claim that people who suffer with repeated battles of constipation are emotionally uptight, and unconsciously refuse to let their bowels go for fear of losing control of something. This is not to say that all constipation is rooted in the above, but consider it. Give up the slave diet and the physical part of this problem diminishes.

Q. 23. I hate to walk barefoot, even if it's on carpet. I have to have something on my feet almost all the time for sanitary purposes.

Answer: FALSE

It has already been explained that because of poor diet many of our ancestors developed chronic diarrhea while aboard the slave ship, and that left untreated the diarrhea was filled with mucus and blood called "the flux." The deck hands made the slaves try to wash and clean up "the flux" they brought up from the hole of the ship or the defecation they expelled while up on deck. The slaves were forced to continue to sleep in this putrid slime below deck to relieve themselves in. And above deck they had to walk and sit in the "flux" because there was no place they could move to. They hated the feel of feces, urine, pus and mucus and blood they were forced to sit and stand in. Then when and if they lived to make it to shore, they had to walk barefoot on the hard and muddy ground until they reached the plantation that would be their permanent home. A strong revulsion to walking barefoot is rooted in "body memories," our feet remember what it was like to walk and stand in sticky filth and since that time have remained uncomfortable walking barefoot – even in the house. The above described condition did not have the same effect on everyone. Sometimes the slaves had to stand, sit and lay in their own excrements for weeks at a time. The Middle Passage trip took from 6 to 8 months barring any inclement weather problems when crossing the Atlantic Ocean from Africa to the states. Sometimes when we get in a serious situation where we feel emotionally threatened we tend to want to break out running – to get away. Symbolic of the many times our ancestors tried to run away from captivity or the anticipation of a beating.

Q. 24. Reading to our children and buying them books for knowledge and entertainment is a very good idea, and we should make sure they have all kinds of literature to keep them interested.

Answer: FALSE

Our slave ancestors commenced to sneak and learn to read around the middle of the 16th century. They figured out a way to listen carefully when the slavemaster or his family members were reading, or sit quietly by when the master's children were being tutored. Of course they had to pretend they were not paying attention but they were. Having no documents or literature from their own tribes, they adapted to English however broken they learned to speak it. Reading and/or writing was only done in secret. Around the 17th century the slaves figured out ways to sneak books or other reading materials out of the house to share with other slaves. There usually were only a few who had figured out how to read so they became the "readers" for the entire group. By the 18th century they had started basic study classes usually convening late at night in some hidden spot. They used makeshift school supplies and all of the books they managed to get their hands on were printed and written by whites and contained European knowledge and featured white characters and lifestyles. It was many years later that Blacks were able to print their own books sometimes featuring Black characters but more often than not they still contained white faces. This, of course, was because by then white skin had become the symbol of beauty, example and purity.

And the only available source of memory we had.

Today we purchase seemingly harmless fairy tale/make believe books sometimes featuring Black characters, and sometimes featuring harmless looking white characters like Snow White, Cinderella, the Little Mermaid, Aladdin or other popular cartoon characters (Beauty & the Beast, etc.). But they are still white people in various disguises and situations being role models and spreading ideas and values. We continue to help our children form opinions of love and admiration for whites while they continue to learn to hate themselves. We are not depriving our children when we prohibit them from reading or owning books and toys featuring caucasians. Books and toys are not harmless, they never have been, they are tools used to teach or form impressions. If we are indeed free, we should stop serving up this poison to our children in the name of popular entertainment. How long is it going to take for us to understand the power and importance of images and words?

Most often it is the Black female mother or guardian who purchases all the clothes and toys for the children in the household. So if you see a little Black girl playing with a white doll, it is because there is a confused Black woman someplace who is helping the enemy destroy our self-image by giving our children Caucasian dolls/toys/games or anything other items with their image on it. We need to see self.

Q. 25. It is unfortunate when Black men or boys stand around and hold their penis. It is an offensive habit and many of them do it to be vulgar, provocative or rebellious.

Answer: FALSE

It is wrong to assume that Black males who tend to grasp, touch or hold on to their penis in public are intentionally trying to be rude or offensive. The motivation for this motion is rooted much deeper than it appears when examined from a "body-language" perspective.

As we already know, the Black males who preceeded us back in slavery time were beaten, branded with hot pokers, chained and castrated. Many of them took to grabbing or holding on to their penis if they were being beaten and not handcuffed or tied. They performed this involuntary movement as a way to protect their private parts from pain. Slave men were encouraged to wear loosely fiited pants so as not to show the imprint of their penis for fear it might be considered as a form of seduction or disrespect to white women or girl children on the plantation. They also tried to play down or hide the imprint of their penis whenever possible because they did not want to anger the master or overseer by reminding them of their own penile inadequacy and provoke envy which might just inspire the master to cut it off by castration. The Black man's penis has always been a part of his anatomy that carries rampant imagination and secret curiosity. Holding on to the penis is another "body memory." Black men when alone among themselves should deal with this topic since the danger described above is no longer a threat to their organ. It would now be more civilized for them to stop this practice and to stop checking to see if it's still there. It is. But since Black males in our ancestry lived so long with the master's perception that their penis was a dangerous weapon, they also may grab their penis as a way to antagonize someone.

Q. 26. When I was a child my neighbors or any other adult in the community could spank me if I was doing something wrong, then tell my parents and sometimes they would whip me again, and it helped me become a better person.

Answer: FALSE

As you should already understand by now, beatings and whippings were the major form of punishment that the slave master and his staff used to force the slaves to submit, to obey – be good and stop rebelling. It is viewed as a source of pride that many of our parents kept us in line and made us respect and obey them by beating our behinds. We laugh about these whippings and often refer back to them and their value in child development. We have often looked on in outrage at Caucasian parents in the mall or on the street who appear to have no control at all over their children. They seem too permissive and weak for letting their children act up so badly in public by allowing them to talk back, throw tantrums or behave unruly uninterrupted – while the parent stands by trying to just talk to the child to calm him down and make him more agreeable. Whew! Sometimes we look away in disgust because we believe all the child needs is a good swat on the butt or whack upside the head.

"Beatings" have become the overall method to employ to control or teach a child right from wrong. The slave master agreed with this process. Our slave ancestors got beat with switches, usually plaited, whips, leather straps and boards. They got beat on the back, buttocks, arms or legs for any infraction as deemed by the master. Members of the House of Commons wrote documents that say "some slave beatings contain circumstances too horrible to be given to the world" so no record of these punishments are available. The master thought that beatings produced a better more obedient slave, and we think that this same method produces better and more obedient children, so we persist in using this technique copying the slave master's idea. More investigation should be given to using nonviolent forms of discipline.

We call it discipline but a child sees it as being attacked by a larger/bigger entity (mom-dad-etc.) so they get hysterical. We need to revisit our ideas of spanking and try to formulate some guidelines that can be taught –especially to new mothers and old people who are raising children and still believe in "beating," or using a "switch" to punish a child.

Q. 27. Although we are not a monolithic people, we are all Black, and we will eventually come together in unity because our needs are the same.

Answer: FALSE

Don't hold your breath. It is unlikely that all of the Black people in America will even come together in agreement about any one issue in our lifetime. This impossibility exists, not only because we disagree with each other on all large issues and fine points on any topic, but we are basically unable to see everything out of the same eye because many of us come from different places. Slaves were captured from such exotic locations in Africa as the Gold Coast, the Congo, Angola, Senegal, large spans of the Eastern and Western coasts (and of course throughout the Caribbean). To just mention a few of the many nations who arrived on these shores, they were Yorubas, Akeans, Ibos, Whydahs, Nagoes, Mandingoes, Koromantyns, Fidahs and Congoes. OBviously this list is not nearly the complete range of Blacks enslaved, they are only a brief example. Each of these nationalities from different areas and territories had different political views, facial characteristics, religions, values, cultures and traditions. While sometimes slave masters would try to routinely purchase slaves from the same tribes so that the slaves he already had could indoctrinate the new slaves coming in as to what the new deal was. Slave documents list the initial impressions of the personalities from some of the above mentioned tribes. They describe the members of these "parcels" as obedient, strong, populous, mean, crafty, smart, fat, stupid, gloomy, impatient, unteachable, lazy, ferocious, stubborn, unruly, rebellious and thievish. We are the descendants of all of these various groups and have different blood lines whose ideas and attitudes are deeply buried in our genetic traits reborn. The slaves who lived to arrive were distributed among the West Indies, New England, the Virginias, New York, the Carolinas and New Orleans for starters. Tribal members are still attracted to each other today. So mass unity is out.

Q. 28. I think women should work outside the home as long as they have good, safe and affordable day care for their children.

Answer: FALSE

Mothers leaving their children in group settings with other children who are not related to them (Nurseries or Day Care Centers) was derived from the slave mother having to leave her babies and small children in baby pools run by one or two other Black women, either too old to work in the field, or in post-partum still nursing. The slave mother was forced to leave the baby with the "sitter" because it slowed up her picking in the fields and took too much time for her to stop and nurse during the work day. The pictures of Black women working in the cotton fields with their babies tied to their backs, which looks like a humane privilege, was a rarity, because actually they had to leave the babies back in the quarters with someone else. Nursing babies was a community service and could be provided by any female of child bearing age who was a mother. More white women than Black have always been afforded the luxury of staying home with their children if they so desired to personally raise them and be in charge of their development. This is not to suggest that white women are the model, because during slavery the master's wife (mistress of the plantation) was so into being pampered and so vain that she refused to even breast feed her own baby. This important bonding process was assigned to a female slave forced to manufacture milk in her own breast to nurse the baby of her oppressor. This is one of the reasons it became popular for us to feed cow's milk to our babies, since the "mistress" fed slave's milk to hers. We just took the same process to a lower direction and applied it to an animal.

The Day Care Centers and Nurseries we have today are inadequate to the emotional and social needs of our children. Not because they are unsafe or too expensive, but because the staff is not being made up of the right entities. Day Care Centers are usually considered as women's territory where females comfortably gather to swap stories, share personal information and exercise complete control over the environment. This is wrong. More Black men need to be involved in Day Care Centers so that those eight to 10 hour days children spend in the care of people outside the home will realistically reflect society and life. These babies need daily interaction with both men and women to develop normally. Men need to work in Day Care Centers as care givers, teachers, feeders, story tellers and administrators. Black babies need to see mother and father images taking care of them, holding them and attending to their needs. Most men don't spend a lot of time with their children in the evening when they get off from work. Weekends are a little better when they get a chance to relate to them in practical activities – doing things or going places. Babies and small children need to see Black men and Black women functioning as both providers and nurturers. Most Day Care Centers are designed exclusively to appeal to women. We need Black men qualified and willing to work in Day Care Centers. And there still remains no better place for a Black child to be than at home with its mother – and father – working in unity to raise the child.

It is conceivable that we need to have standards of dress even for our children in Day Care Centers because as noted before in this text, it is the Black woman who is predominantly in charge of dressing the children in the household and our little girls are dressing to grown-up. Thy look like miniature adults with their little tight jeans, short-shorts and halter tops, along with earrings that are too large for a little girl and high heel sandals which are inappropriate for the development of tiny feet. Wearing a uniform will take the attention away from fashion and put it back on modesty and neatness for girls and boys.

Q. 29. As long as a man takes care of his home obligations, there's nothing wrong with him going out a lot.

Answer: FALSE

Our men seem to be outdoor or away-from-home creatures of habit. They appear somewhat driven to expand on their borders. Constantly. Home often is a place to eat, sleep, change and see a woman. Other than that, unless he is sick or hiding out, he feels compelled to desert the crib and check out the atmosphere elsewhere. Of course many of our men have women or wives who are not with that program so they make it a bit more difficult for them to just up and leave on undefined journeys to unstated destinations. But given a choice, Black men would rather have absolute freedom of motion – to leave.

Overcrowding was always a problem in the slave quarters. They had to live in 10'x14' to 8'x12' huts or shanties. One side of the room usually contained a fireplace for cooking and warmth, there was if attainable a table, maybe a broken chair or stoop of some sort, a couple of windows, a few pots, kettle and lids and blankets on the floor for sleeping or some other type of crude cot. There was absolutely no privacy available. The toilets or toilet area was always outside. It was hot in the summer and cold in the winter and they had only one room. One medium size room that often had to house from six to 10 people, mostly children. While the females of the household had many in-home chores or other domestic activities, it was the males who tended to leave that tiny abode to wander around the grounds (within specified limits) searching for something to do, see or get. The weariness of working all day in the fields still left him with left-over time that he had to fill, and that time was better filled in some wide open space, outdoors, rather than in the house sitting in a corner on the floor, or getting in the way of the women. So today that habit, ingrained during slavery, makes them want to spend the bulk of their time outside the home.

Q. 30. I think Black men blow too much money on clothes, jewelry and cars, but as long as they properly provide for their families, they should have the little extras that make them happy.

Answer: FALSE

During slavery our ancestors received a stipend of about $40.00 per year – which was for everything. They never actually got this full sum in hand, but $40 is what it cost to maintain a slave during the 16th-17th-18th centuries providing them with shelter, food and clothes. With no real weekly paycheck and no real contribution or control over family finances, whenever a slave, the males in particular, got their hands on any extra little tidbit, be it cash or product, they tended to spend or consume it instantly. They were robbed of using their customary forms of barter and exchange which they used in Africa, and the new monetary system was not available to them because of their slave status, so whenever they got anything that even remotely resembled the white man's economic system they delighted in their accomplishment and enjoyed the temporary illusion of having "a plenty." They were trained to live from day to day, with no plans for tomorrow, since tomorrow was preplanned by the master and they had no control over the future either – never knowing what it would bring. The rule for southern slaves in the Louisiana Code of Practice, Article 102 said: "The earnings of slaves and the price of their service belongs to their owners, who have their action to recover the amount of those who have employed them." Furthermore, "Slaves cannot dispose of or receive by donation 'inter vivos or mortis causa'." Article 1462. So it was out of the question for a slave to earn any money and keep it. If a slave managed, with the master's permission, to hire himself out, he had to at least make a quarter for the day, and give the master 15¢ of that. And if some other white person tricked him and got him to work for nothing, he got beat when he got back to the plantation. So the slaves spent fast to keep from having it taken.

Q. 31. Having "Family Reunions" was one of the first new traditions our slave ancestors established to honor the family unit.

Answer: TRUE

The yearly meetings of family members to commemorate their family ties, have big dinners and outdoor bar-be-ques, pray together, have parties, introduce new members of the family and just enjoy each other's company did not begin after slavery ended. It started early during slavery and was referred to as "a gathering." These "gatherings" were linked to sad late night times when friends and other relatives in the slave quarters rallied round when a certain member of another family was sold off by the slave master, or sent away to a far off place to work for another white plantation owner. The "gathering" was a way for other slaves to express their concern and offer emotional support to the grieving family. Being sold off to another slave master was paramount to death and it was such a dreadful occasion that it was generally viewed as a death since it was unlikely that the sold-off family member would ever be seen again. The slaves were considered as chattel – animals, and thus were sold, mated and punished like animals. The "gatherings" were mournful sessions of helplessness that often lasted late into the night, and every effort was made to comfort the family and help them adjust to their loss. This tradition flourished and today family reunions are joyous occasions often complimented with T-shirts, souvenirs, family portraits and happy announcements of births and other familial advancements. Slavery was such a traumatic event in our history that it can be compared to erasing the tapes on a computer, causing us to forget and disavow any previous history prior to 400 years ago. Everything we know about our past now has been provided to us by records, reports and summaries chronicled by others giving eye-witness accounts on paper as to what really happened.

Q. 32. Hypertension, or high-blood pressure, is a medical problem that blacks are genetically predisposed to have, no matter how well we take care of ourself.

Answer: TRUE

Based on extensive review of ships' logs and other documents, Thomas Wilson, Ph.D. and Clarence Grim, Ph.D. of the Hypertension Research Center at the Charles R. Drew University of Medicine and Science in Los Angeles say: "The only slaves who survived the appalling sweat-drenched conditions after capture were those whose kidneys naturally retained large stores of salt. The survivors passsed on this trait, one of the major causes of hypertension to succeeding generations." Wilson and Grim estimate "that massive salt loss contributed to the death of up to 70% of the 12 million African Blacks who were pressed into slavery between the 16th and 19th centuries." Many slaves also suffered from massive salt loss from their bodies on the long shackled marches from the African interior, before even boarding the slave ship. After capture and on board the slave ship, all slaves with the physical capacity to retain salt in their bodies were more apt to survive the ordeal of captivity. And due to the brutality of the abduction of our ancestors we have inherited this genetic predisposition to having hypertension. Many symptoms of this condition can be controlled and managed with a better diet, routine exercise and a less stressful existence. The medication Black men are required to take to control hypertension has an increased risk of creating impotency, so many men stop taking their blood pressure medication because of the diminishing of their sexual capacity. Hopefully one of our scientists will discover a homeopathic or organic medication that will have better results than the dangerous synthetic drugs now offered. Almost 30 percent of Blacks age 18 to 74 have hypertension and it runs in families prone to heart disease.

We have the stress of loneliness', the stress of not having an abundance of material goods and the stress of being generally embarrassed about our condition, the car we drive, where we live, etc.

Answer: TRUE

We do. On the ships coming over, salt was the most effective preservative to keep meats and fish from spoiling and was used as a universal practice on the ships and on the plantation. Salt was also the ample condiment used on the plantations to alter the taste of the rough green leaves and vegetables that made up the slave diet. Cayenne pepper was also used to season cooked foods and for medicinal purposes. Although the slave master viewed the slave as a combination of animal and machine which he needed to work the fields for him and perform domestic duties for he and his family; he did not take good care of his slave. He took more time caring for his prized dogs and horses and his farm animals than his slaves. Food was plentiful on the plantation as a rule so the masters' tables were always brimming with meals featuring several courses. The meats consisted of mainly pork cooked in several ways and chicken. Mostly fried chicken. The slave cooks managed to steal little tid-bits of food and hide them beneath their aprons or hand them out the window to waiting accomplices to be consumed later by their family. During the 1500's and up into the 1600's the slaves were given the lowest of rations, rotten food and sparse clothing. Many of the slaves, unable to work the long field shifts, became ill and died from poor nutrition. This convinced the slave master to provide them with better food. It had nothing to do with the slave master to provide them with better food. It had nothing to do with the slave master desiring to share his bounty or make the slaves happier. His motivation for giving the slaves better food was purely selfish and financially based. He did not like the idea of losing out on his investment (the cost of the slave) based on the slave dying at a young age. As the food allotments improved, gardens and hunting were permitted; the heavy usage of salt and cayenne continues to be a seasoning habit even to this day.

Q. 34. Most of our men are frightened and antagonistic about the responsibilities of marriage and fatherhood.

Answer: TRUE

Black fathers, like Black mothers, love their children and share the same desire to have a home and family. They do not repel this commitment based on an innate dislike of the family unit. The Black man's ego (self-esteem) is so fragile that he rejects any situation which targets his inabilities or shortcomings. He is overly sensitive to failure and their disenfranchisement both educationally and economically further weakens his drive to become a part of a family unit. Even if he knows that his woman knows that he is treated unfairly in the work force, his own frustration is based on the seemingly hopeless situation of his not being able to provide for his family. This knowledge, whether real or imagined, speeds up his abandonment of any attempt to sustain a family. Men continue to view economic dependency as a guarantee of fidelity in women and to validate their authority in a marriage. They also see economic dependency on a subconscious level as a way to keep their Black woman out of the employ of white males. They view the financial support of their family as a protective measure that women don't usually understand. The weakening of their husband and father position was instigated by the poor behavior of other men, the feminist movement advocating equality of the sexes and other contemporary issues that question his masculine authority and personal values. All of this makes him feel devalued and his social role pattern has been dismantled mainly due to economics. Now he just won't deal, and he knows for a fact that the advances that Black women seem to make are merely attempts by white males to keep them subordinate. If money is the measure then he knows he can't compete. So he has to convince himself that he doesn't want to settle down and have a family anyway. And he has to convince himself that supporting babies is not really his problem. He disconnects mentally, emotionally and spiritually from childbirth and child rearing because this is an area in which he has no real control. He can't stand the weight. The pressure is too much. Some Black men have overcome these obstacles. This is pretty much the same posture and attitude that our ancestral Black men in slavery had. From the moment they boarded the ship they were no longer in a position to care for, protect or provide for their wives and family. He had no authority even over himself in the new world of slavery. On the plantation his only value was that of common laborer and his agility as a stud. His woman had several uses; she was valued as cook, housekeeper, nursemaid and other general "mammy" duties. Plus, even if against her will, she had the capability to be used as a sex object by the master, his sons and associates. The Black male slave had none of the "natural privileges" he had in his homeland and he was prevented from protecting his women and girls from rape attacks, being sold on the auction block or submitting to any and all whims of any white male in view. Any attempts to protect his women, any protest whatsoever, elicited an immediate unmerciful beating, maiming or being killed on the spot. With no right to even visit his slave family without permission from the master – he withdrew, developing a blind side to the dangers imposed on his women since he couldn't do anything about it anyway. The obligations of marriage were inconsistent with the rules of slavery. His contribution to a relationship during slavery was random and unpredictable. And it remains that way to this very day. These feelings of inadequacy and helplessness have been transmitted through his genes into his sperm and is now fully reproduced, to the across-the-board dismay of Black women all over the country.

Black men of adequate age were bred to breed, so it is no wonder that he goes from place to place impregnating women and moving on seemingly forgetting all about them and the child.

Q. 35. Blacks tend to be more prone to pulmonary heart problems and respiratory diseases of breathing moreso than whites.

Answer: FALSE

It may sound pretty farfetched but European medical scientists back in the late 1800's claimed they discovered through anthropological studies that Blacks were physiologically ill-suited for cold weather. They say that we, as natives of tropical climates exclusively, have lungs unable to properly inhale and exhale such cold dry atmosphere as such exists in North America. Other medical observations showed that Black slaves slept with their heads next to the fire and required blankets to keep from shivering from the cold temperatures during long witners on the plantation. They saw this as a sign that we were attracted to warmth and moisture in order to breathe easier. One study pointed out that before we came to live around caucasians we were not susceptible to bacterial pneumonias. Whites in America were prone to long bouts of yellow fever, malaria and measles more than slaves. Also the overcrowding and unsanitary living conditions intermingled with the cold drafty cabins allowed the slaves to be exposed to more airborne infections. Respiratory illnesses among the first slaves to arrive were rampant, and remained so for as long as the slaves had to work outdoors all seasons year round. Frostbite was another problem of adjusting to the cold weather in America. Many slaves lost limbs, toes or fingers from contacting frostbite at sea on the slave ship. The South Africans working the gold mines there, having moved from an inland more tropical location, are also recorded to contact pneumonia more than the whites in that area. Today many of us are constantly cold, having never adjusted to the severe climate we find ourselves stuck in. Whites seem to enjoy frigid temperatures and have several recreational activities involving snow, ice and brittle cold weather. Not us. Most would never consider taking a cruise to Alaska for a vacation like some of them do.

Q. 36. It may not be discussed as much anymore, but I still think some Black mothers prefer their daughters to marry a light-skinned African-American or even a white man.

Answer: TRUE

After our ancestors accepted the unflinching reality of their new life in America that commenced to adapt to the social mores, customs, culture and values of the whites they were surrounded by. The values and lifestyle of the whites was all they saw as being worthy of emulation. The only other world they had to compare to the one whites represented was their own morbid life of drudgery in the slave quarters. Given that nearly every tradition practiced in Africa was forgotten after a few generations, the slave remembered nothing else to compare the white man's ideas to. After "white" was accepted as the level of status to strive for, along with it came an internal color classification among the slaves. It was impossible for them not to notice that any slaves sired by the master or other white men, looked remarkably different than the rest of them. The children of mixed parentage had thinner lighter hair, colorful eyes and some of the prized lighter skin (almost like whites) that had such great value around them. The fairer skinned slaves garnered more house assignments, were somewhat favored by the master, and sometimes lived in absolute luxury as compared to the rest of the slaves. The slave mothers eventually saw opportunity in their daughters attracting a white man and becoming his mistress. They saw it as a way to keep their child from having to perform hard labor in the fields. These matings and the children resulting from them had a greater chance for better treatment because they contained precious white blood. They had several color differentiations: musteefino, mustee, quad-roon, octaroon and mulatto. If a mulatto (racial mixture of white and black) became impregnated by a regular African slave, their offspring was known as a "Sambo." The greatest success that the Black slave mother could hope for was that often the white father of a mixed child would grant it freedom. This was usually done when the child reached adolescence. Needless to say, the Mulatto-Quadroon-Octaroon (very fair skinned Blacks sometimes two generations up from their Africanism) had higher self-esteem and believed themselves to be better than the regular "darkies" on the plantation with their blackened skin and crinkly nappy hair. They would sometimes treat the dark skinned negroes as badly or worse than the whites if they were in such a position to do so. They were ashamed to be even remotely related to the common field slave or domestic worker. They felt their improved status from having white blood and white facial features launched them several steps above the other slaves. Class distinction had begun, based on color, neighborhood, education and material riches. This has not changed.

Today, shamefully, many of these same attitudes prevail between the light skinned Blacks and the dark skinned Blacks, and the Blacks who are successful and those who are not. Black mothers from the old school say they do not mind if their daughters (or sons) marry a caucasian. They claim it doesn't matter as long as their daughter is happy and he treats her good. This is a hold-over slave prayer that perhaps their daughter will achieve the social standing she is worthy of – a social advancement that will propel her into another category of existence, and hopefully deliver up little pointed-nose children with "good" hair and light eyes. This marrying "up" procedure is still looked upon in disdain by the ordinary negroes who see no way to improve the color shade or hair texture of their kin. This explanation is not an attempt to oversimplify or stereotype our views on this topic, but these ideas still remain and the class distinction has held fast, even if the color issue has abated. Classification for value is still based on education, neighborhood, title and material riches. All of these attitudes came out of our slave history. We should end them.

Q. 37. Unfortunately, some of us are back-stabbers, we sneak behind each other and do negative things, and care little about loyalty if the price or benefit of disloyalty is worth it.

Answer: TRUE

The disloyalty we practice against each other takes place with strangers, our friends and family. Sometimes we are known to do things so dispicable against each other that onlookers are shocked. Sometimes we hold grudges against each other for years and uphold practices of feudalism between families for often decades on end. We will sneak behind each other and report discrepancies or tardiness to the boss on the job. We will tell husbands information about their wives, and visa-versa, and start marital problems between them. We spread false rumors to get someone in trouble or expelled from a group or organization. We call these examples disunity but the roots of "back-stabbing" go deeper than that.

When the slave trade business began almost all European nations tried to capitalize on this new commodity worth immediate cash money. The majority of the ship mates who hired on for voyages to capture slaves in Africa were social outcasts, derelicts, unskilled and poor laborers with strong stomachs for violence. They first just pillaged the coast raiding villages and seizing lone natives in the jungles along the coasts. This was timely, undependable and hard on the ship mates who were not used to the food, insects and climate. Soon, the captain and his administrative staff recognized a more viable system whereby they would capitalize on the politics of the jungle. They sought out warring tribes and found chiefs who were willing to sell captives of other tribes they had defeated in wars. Dissatisfaction over hunting grounds, waterways, land, religion, government and law had already created separate nations and languages. This made it easier for the Europeans to go in and instigate wars and break the peace among them – then they would approach the winning tribe and offer them trinkets and amazing supplies from Europe and the Americas. This is how they convinced the various African tribes to turn against each other, and sell each other for gold and material gain. The African leaders, chiefs and warlords, were happy to get rid of their competition and relieved at not having to worry about them coming back to attack them in the future. After this kind of delivery system was set up the Africans were designated agents of the Europeans and assigned the task of going into the interior up and down the Guinea Coast to round up slaves. The African bounty hunters learned to operate the ankle and wrist irons, which held better than rope, hemp or vine. They would march their captive prisoners to the shores, mistreating them with switches they made and whips provided by the Europeans. As the word traveled from tribe to tribe via complex communication systems, that certain other Africans were getting luxuries such as gold, clothes, jewelry, umbrellas, music boxes, hats, mirrors and a plethora of trinkets never seen on the continent before. Then members of various communities started doing anything they could to get some of the new products. They would charge their mates with infidelities, others were pointed out as robbers, while still others were so poor from famine they sold their own children. The more vicious of the Africans took to kidnapping other Blacks and personally sold them to the Europeans. Of course, due to the greedy nature of the traders they would often accept the kidnapped Black and then overpower the Black person who turned him in and chain them together and put them on the ship – both bound for slavery in America. The seed of these African "back-stabbers" is also scattered among us – many still causing similar types of discord in their own homes and communities. They are the ones who spy or infiltrate Black organizations or groups to go back and report to the "master" what's going on. They are called "traitors" or "defectors."

Q. 38. Although camping is not necessarily my idea of fun, I do like to attend outdoor religious services when the weather is really hot.

Answer: TRUE

Practicing any kind of religion, either African or christian, was prohibited among our ancestors. They were beaten or punished severely for trying to hold on to any remnants of African spirituality, and prevented by law from adopting christianity. Meeting in groups for religious purposes was initially illegal because it bordered on the laws against negro slaves receiving "mental instruction." If they were allowed to visit a christian church meeting there had to be several whites in attendance, or even worse, the sermon had to be given by a white pastor who preached on the goodness fo slavery among other things. Along with the eventual permission for Black slave ministers to hold church meetings, was the obstacle of finding a place large enough to hold church services in. In addition, it remained a requirement that these meetings not be held in private. Thus the idea of using "tents" solved both problems. "Tents" were raised everywhere negro slaves congregated. Along with this preview of "freedom of religion" came the option of choosing which type of christianity the slave wanted. This was usually a choice between baptist and methodist. These "tent" grounds often supplied ample space for two "open house" churches, one for each religion. Each slave minister competed with the other in preaching. They vied to be the one who extracted the most converts from the audience, and yelled, sweated and stomped to stir up repentance. This also allowed any nearby whites to hear what they were saying and think it was just harmless fire and brimstone christianity paganized by the darkies. Sometimes whites stood around outside the tents and watched the shouting and wild antics going on non-stop all day. Today some of our evangelical or revival services are held each year during warm seasons outside in "tents" which are open to the public to attend.

Christianity has not saved us – it never did. Many of the onlookers and participants in the lynching of Blacks in America were pastors/preachers/ministers and the like. They did not intervene in the name of Christianity to save us.

Work is for weekdays, but the weekend, especially Saturday night, is for relaxing or party-time.

Answer: TRUE

Our slave ancestors worked from the first light of the sun until late evening, sometimes up to around 10:00pm at night. The work week could run from Monday to Sunday, or Monday to Friday, which was the usual 80 to 100 hour work week. The slave masters all agreed that the slaves revealed a seemingly inborn need to dance, make music and practice merriment – despite their life of work, brutality and scorn. The master grew to recognize that the slaves appeared to work better and have overall better spirit for work if he allowed them a little time every week to dance and have fun as they knew it. He saw their eagerness for display of their physical abilities, fancy clothes and bright colors. So the master began encouraging them in their miniscule attempts to relax and let off a little steam. He chose for them Saturday night into Sunday morning to use for their "party" time and he dedicated that night to be their official celebration time. And we have used Saturday nights for that purpose ever since then.

Every holiday, special day or festivity that we have invented is somehow rooted in our slave history, related to it or based on something about it, because we have no memories or connections to anything we did to celebrate prior to that time. So even when we reject the formal holidays created by European thought, at the present we have nothing of our own to replace it with. And the only convivial affairs we have adopted are all, when traced, an outgrowth of our slavery past. Slavery ended everything holy or happy for us. The reason the Jews, Japanese and Indians have not suffered the kind of stunting development we have is that their captors did not force them to abandon their cultural practices. The Jews were permitted to maintain their religion and practices, the Indians were allowed to keep their tribal customs and symbols, and the Japanese were not prevented from speaking their own language and practicing their traditions. <u>We were stripped of everything</u>.

The most prized colored outfit to wear to one of these Saturday night dances or parties was a red hat, red shirt, red dress or red ribbon or rag on the head. A few historians mention that the color red was a favorite color among the slaves, and that red cloth was one of the gifts used to trick the Africans into following the Europeans down to the harbor where the slave ship awaited. Apparently there was no bright red fabrics along the West coast of Africa, which is the primary area from which the slave traders captured their prey. Offerings of red cloth was a great enticement because it was so unusual and new to them. Later on we developed a habit of laughing at dark skinned Blacks who wore red, thinking they were too "dark" to wear such a bright color. But lately during the past couple of years with the re-resurrection of African styled clothing and bright African kente colors, it has become more in fashion to wear bright red colors based on its popularity.

Q. 40. When working for white companies' Black supervisors (bosses) tend to be more strict on other Black employees than a white person holding a similar management position.

Answer: TRUE

On the plantation where our ancestors worked, they did not always perform voluntarily. It was hot, hard, backbreaking labor that went on non-stop except for a couple of 20 minute breaks. To solve their nonmotivation the slave master hired an "Overseer" who could be either agriculturally astute or a member of the "po white trash" who lived on one of the poorer farms nearby. The overseer kinda rode shotgun over the slave workers, usually on horseback, and he carried both a gun and cowhide whips. The gun to protect himself from slave insurrection or any attempt to overthrow the field system, and the whip to lash out and sting the back, head or neck of any slave moving too slow or who without authorization sat down to rest.

The other official in the field was called a "Slave Driver" and he was usually chosen from among the slaves for his meanness or impatience with the other slaves. Or he might be chosen for his strength or knowledge of planting. The slave driver was also in charge of metering out punishment when directed to by the overseer. He had no real power and could be flogged himself if he appeared to be going too easy on another slave who he had been told to whip. Long drawn out punishments were not the norm, punishments usually were sharp, impromptu and informal. The slave driver had to always make sure, in order to protect himself, that he mistreated the other slaves to the satisfaction of the overseer and the master. He had to make sure that he did not show favoritism to the slaves just because he was a slave too. Today many Blacks in supervisory, management or administrative positions function the same way. They like to demonstrate to their white bosses that they hold no special consideration or favoritism to other Blacks subordinate to them. They want to be seen as impartial and nonbiased. They are strident in their job performance reviews of other Blacks and make every effort to be nondenominational regarding race affiliation. They want their white boss to feel comfortable and assured by proof that they are not racially slanted or influenced. The Black "slave driver" was also allowed to come to the front porch or back of the house if the master summoned him. Many slaves lived their entire lives never getting within 100 feet of the "big house" and could only rely on reports from the "in-house" slaves about the kind of furniture or chandeliers contained in the "big house." The slave driver was proud of those occasions when he was commanded to come up to the "big house." He felt proud, it was comparable to the commendatory pat on the head that the master reserved for his favorite slaves. It was this approval and acceptance that many slaves lived for. Today many of us still experience a thrill when invited to the "big house" and it is announced in all of our papers, on the radio and T.V. None of us have ever been summoned to the "big house" (in Washington, D.C.) and refused to go. It is considered a mark of pride and grand achievement.

> **Q. 41.** We should not reject the European style marriage ceremony just because we like more cultural rituals at our weddings.

Answer: TRUE

Certainly it makes sense that we would want to redesign the current Europeanized wedding ceremony because we are a creative people and like to do things our own way. But what we have usually replaced it with is not from our own creativity. Many of us are now hosting elaborate weddings dressed in traditional African garb and participate in the entertaining and delightful event of "jumping the broom." Well, this activity may seem cute and original, but it is not. In the first place our ancestors in Africa did not have or jump brooms to get married. Our slave ancestors in America did not devise the procedure of "jumping the broom" to get married either. If a slave man wanted to get married, the slave man would not go to the girl's parents, he would have to go and ask the slave master about it. The master would either say yes or no on the spot, or contact the girl in question. If her answer was affirmative, he would inform the slave man and a wedding date was set. Since the Slave Laws at that time prohibited slaves from marrying, the slave master could not, in good conscience, permit the slaves to enjoin by following the rules of christian marriage, which was only reserved for whites. Slaves were considered 'chattel' and 'chattel' do not marry. The "Federal Congress" of the day which dealt with such matters concluded that "Slaves are not people in the eye of the law. They have no legal personality. The slave is not ranked among sentient beings, but among things, and things are not married." If a slave was allowed to marry according to white contractual laws, it meant that the slave was then free. Left with the task of devising a tradition that was symbolic but not legal, the slave masters came up with the "jumping the broom" ritual. This was done in one of two ways. Either the slave couple was commanded to jump over the broom then turn around and jump back; or the couple joined hands and jumped backwards over a broomstick, then the master would pronounce them married. Sometimes these wedding celebrations lasted all night and the master would provide extra food and corn whiskey to commemorate the occasion. The wedding night was often interrupted when and if the mistress or master needed the new bride or groom to do some chore up at the big house. The couple lived together.

These wedding receptions and other parties also gave rise to the use of bright red ribbons, pieces of string or fabric in the hair. On the plantation there were no straightening combs, hot irons or perms. The women treasured every swatch of colored fabric they got their hands on. Most of their clothes were gray, brown, black or beige. Being female, they too desired colorful adornments. The only thing available to fix their children's hair or their own was scarves received from the mistress, or long strips they wrapped around their heads as a turban. But what many of them loved the most was parting their child's hair, or their own, in separate strands and tying red strips of cloth, about the width of silk ribbon, around each clump of hair all over the head. Most of the "pickaninnies" on the plantation (the small children) wore strings of this multi-colored cloth tied all over their heads. There are many nostalgia dolls modeled after that time with little Black heads covered with 10 or more tiny red ribbons in the hair. This memory is manifested today as we see little Black girls all over America with a head full of different colored barrettes, each attached to a different plait or pony tail. Their Black mothers think it is just a cute hair style and do not realize that this style of hair dressing is rooted in their ancestral slave history.

Q. 42. Riots and social upheavals are terrible but they are a political option we use to express rebellions and let off a little steam.

Answer: TRUE

We have never participated in a riot in the entire time we have been in America which elicited an immediate change of conditions towards the better for us. Our riots are in our own neighborhoods, displace the members of our own community and we are penalized further by the slowness of the legal system both in rebuilding and providing emergency needed aid. What we destroy may not be ours, but it certainly comprises what we use and need. Riots are not a new form of rebellion for us. Our slave ancestors instigated what the master called "slave rebellions" on the plantations. They would burn their shanties, burn the crops and try to infiltrate and burn the master's house also. Their riots/ rebellions failed then for the same reasons ours fail now. The whites were the majority, were better organized, better armed, strategically educated on war and controlled the food and water. The master was reassured that no matter what, he had the most bullets. The slave master was not a fool, and he knew that the potential for slave rebellions was great, his knowledge of any mini-rebellions close by was up to date and remembered every waking hour. He knew that the hard work, humiliation, beatings and confinement of the slaves made them resent and hate him even if they stood daily grinning in his face. It developed in him a paranoia he deemed well founded. Because he knew how badly he treated his slaves, he could never be sure they would keep taking it, and it made him suspicious and distrustful of blacks. And this suspicion and distrust lives on today among whites. They can never really be sure they are free from the threat of revenge, or that we are really honest when we say 'let bygones be bygone.' The slaves love-hate relationship with the master kept him on his toes. After all he had pious, delicate and saintly white women and children to protect, and strong, arrogant, handsome sons who were to be his heirs.

Marches are only good as a tool to allow us to let off steam, have something to do and put our bodies in motion to demonstrate our solidarity of disagreement. However, all of that "HANDS UP DON'T SHOOT! And "I CAN'T BREATHE," and "NO JUSTICE NO PEACE" is ALLLLL totally useless!!! Not one white person in power cares about us marching. And when our fearless youth turn the march into a physical protest they are charged with being thugs and robbers.

All damage that a protester does during an uprising is considered collateral damage during war.

> **Q. 43.** Black churches are now becoming more racially mixed (multicultural) not because whites want to integrate but because they like our joyful singing, music and energetic services.

Answer: TRUE

No way. Whites today consider a religious and bible-bearing black espousing christian values less of a threat than an atheistic dissatisfied negro with no God conscience, or one following some eastern paganism with secret rituals. During slavery when our ancestors were finally allowed to preach and follow the christian doctrines, they were not given the entire bible at one time, because the slave masters did not want the slaves to find out about the parts in the bible that said things like, "He that stealeth a man and selleth him, or if he be found in his hand, he shall surely be put to death," (Exodus xxi 16:) so the master withheld the Old Testament until he was assured that the slaves were so deeply committed and fearful of the christian God that they would not misinterpret some of the passages against slavery. Also the master needed time to depersonalize the parables in the bible so the slave would not recognize himself in its teachings. Another way to keep tabs on the religious development of the slaves was to personally attend their church services, or to have a white preacher open up the meetings and give the proper interpretations of the bible. Both of these systems turned out to be more appealing and entertaining that the master originally thought. The white community's religious services were boring and ineffective when compared to the loud rantings, foot-tapping music, shouting and wild gyrations that went on in slave worship. Whites have always attended our churches, and sadly, we have always been proud to have them there. All God's children together worshipping and praying to one God – theirs. Whites like the "life" and "passion" we bring to everything we do, and it is addictive to them, and becomes a form of release they are unfamiliar with which can be practiced among other whites in agreement, or blacks who don't matter.

Q. 44. It is okay if my children go out and tell others what I talk about at home, and I should not reprimand or chastise them for repeating publicly what I say in private.

Answer: TRUE

One of the first social lessons regarding behavior outside the home is that we teach our children to keep their mouth shut about whatever goes on in the house. We will spank them as soon as we get the chance if we have taken them someplace with us and they start mouthing off about something we said, or said about somebody, back at home. We also remind them to "stop looking in my mouth" meaning for them to stop paying attention to everything I say. Or "I better not hear this no more, you don't say nothin' to nobody about what we say in here." This came from an old custom among our slave ancestors which they started to keep their children from saying things around the master that would get them in trouble. Slave mothers had to be very severe with their young children to make them understand the seriousness of not telling what went on at home, and not talking too much when they were out playing with the master' children. This instruction was also given to the children because the parents knew that the master or the mistress would try to get the slave children to, in effect, spy on their parents or the other adult slaves, with the promise of some trinket or tidbit. Many a slave was beaten half-to-death because of some seemingly innocent remark made by a slave child about its parents. This instruction is still used today as part of our teachings on manners. We tell our children it is impolite or not in good taste to repeat what the adults say to other people. The simple solution to this problem, if it is one, is to stop saying things around the children that we don't want them to repeat. They are like little sponges and soak up everything they see or hear, and it is not fair to penalize them for our own improper indiscretions. Let us not keep perpetuating the same slavery techniques generation after generation.

We now have national proof that we made a huge mistake in not forming our own schools. Today the media teaches our children more than schools do.

Q. 45. True, we are up from slavery, free and have more rights than ever before, but we must remember that we are still hostages.

Answer: TRUE

Our slave ancestors were first taken hostage in order to get them aboard the slave ship, pack them like sardines below deck, and force them to live in filth in the dark for weeks on end. Psychologists call such terroristic treatment as "sensory deprivation," when an individual is deprived of all normal sensations such as light, food, environment, family and familiar sounds. They say this process causes such deep emotional damage that the mental anguish and lingering terror may take months or years to recover. Although we chose not to identify with this, back in 1986, then Vice-President George Bush released a report by his task force on "Combatting Terrorism." It defined terrorism as "the unlawful use or threat of violence against persons or property to further political or social objectives. It is usually intended to intimidate or coerce a government, individuals or groups to modify their behavior or politics."

We have particularly suffered from attempts to "modify our behavior" ever since day one when our ancestors were stolen and tricked into coming here. The modification process took form as convincing us that we were sentenced to a lifelong existence of dependency, discrimination, rejection and powerlessness from being displaced and robbed of our preslavery memories. And possibly most important the knowledge of the importance and necessity of work for survival. Primal law is that each species provides for and protects itself. We are unable to perform either one of these basic life preserving functions independently.

Our slave ancestors were forced, now we collectively choose to go through life dependent and suffering. Pleading with the white man to repent and revise his system to accommodate our inadequacy. It will never happen.

Q. 46. Sometimes when I am in a small room, crowded elevator or large group of people, I get uncomfortable and start to feel suffocated.

Answer: TRUE

Our slave ancestors were forced to live and sleep below deck in the "hole" of a ship, dehumanized and packed and wedged together as cargo. It was lightless, airless with virtually no ventilation. There was also no windows, no portholes, no cracks; except a square iron rate for going in and out. Sometimes temperatures reached upwards to 120°F, so hot that steam emitted from the grate and it was hot to the touch like an oven. The trip through the famed Middle Passage took between two to six months dependent upon grasping good winds and fair weather. We were piled together horizontally and vertically and bent over. The slaves were loaded so tightly no one could roll over, stand up or bend down. It was a sweaty excrement laced pigsty and it was overcrowded shoulder to shoulder. So it is entirely conceivable that when standing in a room filled with other Blacks, or finding ourself in a windowless small room, that we might re-experience an overpowering feeling of too closeness. An elevator or closet can bring this about.

That's another reason we demand so much respect for "our space," and will tell anyone in no limit of time, "don't be gettin' up in my face." We may even feel uncomfortable if someone stands too close to us and consider it ill-mannered. We don't want to be too close anymore, and it's not because we don't necessarily like each other, it's just that we would rather not be crowded or pressed. And yes, this reaction falls under the "body memory" category of post-traumatic stress subsequent to our slave history. These involuntary flashbacks are an overwhelming feeling. We are not crazy and we are not hallucinating, we are actually having these "in-body" experiences which no one can understand or identify with but us.

This being outdoors a lot is another reason the enemy has so many opportunities to murder our men because no matter what season or weather, there will be pockets of Black men or boys conjugating on street corners or doorsteps talking or just jiving around to be together. Even those brothers doing illegal business are primarily outside.

Q. 47. Even when we complete college, or get skilled training in a specific field to become successful, it still seems like something is missing.

Answer: TRUE

There is an old saying that "It is better to give a poor man a day's work than a day's meal," because one must uphold the principles of individual survival and the prominence of the work before food sequence. We are entirely committed to securing better education to advance our causes. Many of us have excelled in our particular vocational choice at least during some period of our lives. Others of us look with faith and anticipation to a more positive future. We should not forget the masses of us who gain a substantial number of degrees and are unable to maintain or get a job. As it has turned out "work" – having a job, especially working for someone else, it's not all it's pumped up to be. Eventually the routine becomes routine, mundane and something to do, and requires us to become totally absorbed in making a living – however disconnected it may seem in the long run. Having succeeded can even make us sad or ladened with anxiety of unknown origin. We feel like something is missing, but actually what we experience is an overriding grief, a sadness that we have been able to achieve something or get something that our ancestors were denied and never had.

GRIEVING FOR THE CAPTURED, THOSE LOST IN THE MIDDLE PASSAGE, AND THE TORMENTED SOULS TORTURED AND MURDERED IN AMERICA.

Because we have thought that slavery happened so long ago, and now many of us have white blood in our veins, and there are no slaves still living – we have given little consideration to grieving for our enslaved ancestors. It has been more emotionally safe to look back at them as foreigners, removed from family ties, strange and odd looking. But this writing suggests that one of the ways to rid ourselves of the overwhelming pity and anger we feel about how they were brought here, what they endured and how they died; is to hold Afrocentric ceremonies and grieve for them. Or to let it out and grieve for them in private. We owe them and ourselves those tears. Cleansing waterfall tears pent up and only expressed as anger. Tears we have supressed by denial and disassociation. Since coming here we have known but three major emotions – fear, rage and confusion, with all three being reproducible by multiple external stimuli. The one emotion we have not allowed ourselves to vent about slavery, is grief. We must mourn for them. Mourning has been defined as "the reaction to the loss of a loved one, or one's country, liberty or ideal." Our ancestors experienced the loss of all of the above, and we feel that pain, or at least we should feel that pain. Unresolved grief has terrible consequences and it cannot be skipped or avoided because there are several penalties for delaying grief. It manifests as disinterest, dissatisfaction and inhibitions with a loss of capacity to love freely. We can rid ourselves of our intense pining and yearning for them and replace it with commemoration, respect and acknowledgment. Maybe then we can come to grips with our sorrow and move on. Not forgetting them ever, but laying them at peace, so we can be grateful for that black soil we grew out of. By bidding them a proper farewell we free ourselves up to justify their struggle and use their strength as reason to survive.

Q. 48. Melanin, the Black chemical in our skin, is said to contain the entire history of man. We have the most lingering memories because our race has more Melanin than all the others.

Answer: TRUE

Using a brief quick definition, Melanin is the chemical in our skin, eyes and hair which makes us have dark skin color. It is our "Blackness" and carried within it our entire history unfolds. Genetic scientists say Melanin has a pleasant aroma, is thermally structured, and is tough. Obviously Melanin also quantifies our ego because we attribute great things both physically and mentally to it. Melanin cradles our social, cultural and political histories, including what happened to our ancestors in slavery.

Melanin could be grouped scientifically with "Prana." The Honorable Elijah Muhammad, Messenger of Allah, taught that Prana is: "merely a form of energy used by the Black ego in its material manifestation" and "is the universal life principle in all forms and the energies of the Black body are the differentiated quota of that universal principle, which any particular human soul has appropriated."

All people of color have Melanin but we have the most. The slavemasters made up categories to define the amount of Melanin we had in our bodies:

Mangroon	– all Black, full blood
Sambo	– 3/4 Black (this name was also used to refer to a plantation slave who was stupid)
Mulatto	– 1/2 Black blood
Quadroon	– 1/4 Black blood
Octaroon	– 1/8 Black blood
Mestizo	– 1/2 a quarter Black blood

These racial definitions seemed to vary according to state sometimes. Melanin and Prana are heavy complicated topics which are best taught and explained in detail by those specializing in such science.

Today Melanin and our stem cells remain a hot topic of debate because the use of them in healing has been studied and proven to be even greater than anticipated in preventing disease and death. We were programmed during slavery to believe that we were no good but as it turns out; we are not just good, we are the best specimens on earth of human life.

> **Q. 49.** I am not ready or willing to let go of our negative past and look with hope to the future, because I don't see things getting any better.

Answer: TRUE

They're not. We have witnessed a man walking on the moon, celebrated Black History Month and Black Family Day. And we have seen the bravest and most intelligent among us be promoted to high governmental posts. And we have seen the polished look of our families, free to do whatever they choose to do with their lives. It would be in error to say that we have made no progress at all. Yet and still our growth has been sporadic and undependable, and the mathematics to guarantee success for each and every one of us eludes us consistently. No matter how hard we try we just can't get our collective acts together, and we continue to complain complain complain about the system – and each other. The one tie that binds us – discrimination and integration – keeps us confused and unsure about what to do next. Trying to awaken all of our consciousness all at once remains an impossibility. Lewis and Hubbard described our self-consciousness saying that we "draw a fainter line of demarcation between will and destiny, illusion and knowledge, and dreams and facts, and make less distinction between hallucinations and objective existences." We have it all mixed up. Lewis and Hubbard arrived at this conclusion during their stint of research in "Manic Depressive Reactions in Negroes" back in 1931. Unfortunately, this definition is more true than ever today. And who should know better than them, since they are the ones who put us in this condition.

We don't know how to use <u>will</u> to predict destiny.

We misread our 'beliefs' into illusions having no mathematical basis as being true, or even having the potential to one day be true. We think that our dreams represent actual facts dependable and firm. And our goals become hallucinations filled with relief despite all research into our present condition that indicates the opposite.

Wishing and hoping will not help. We have to work for progress.

Q. 50. Even the most militant among us have to admit that all white people are not alike. Despite the fact they share the same nature, some of them express it differently.

Answer: TRUE

The temperament of the slave masters who ruled our ancestors was as varied as the tribes who landed on these shores. There are scant reports that some slave masters actually treated their slaves as somewhat human. They are reported to have allowed their slaves to have as much food as they wanted, marry and live with whom they pleased, and some even permitted their slaves to use their homes for a wedding hall. The master and mistress placed their small children in the care of the hoards of little picka-ninnies, children of the slaves, and possibly treated them as playmates. Some allowed their slaves to attend parties every weekend on other plantations, or visit with their former wives who had been sold away, or gave them real beds and night clothes to sleep in. The master had it at his disposal to educate any child he fathered by a slave, and to free them when they reached adolescence. They would provide retirement privileges to slave workers who had given them 30-40-50 years of unstinting service, and who took abuse uncomplainingly. They defended favorite slaves from the wrath of the Slave Driver. This type of master felt protective over his wards. Naturally today, many of us believe that we know whites who fall into the category of being the "good slave master," and we have ready explanations as to why that particular caucasian is 'not like the rest.' Let us not forget how our ancestors were manipulated into working harder and being better slaves. Some of the masters figured out how to psyche us out, then soon as we believed the hype, we let our guard down and didn't realize how we were being tricked for hidden agenda goals. We have been too psychologically damaged to be able to select the good apple out of the barrel. We are too deeply entrenched in the near psychosis of our post-traumatic stress disorder. This test is to help you first judge your own behavior, then you might be qualified to judge others.

NUMERICAL GRADE INTERPRETATIONS

<u>GRADES of 86 to 100</u>
(up to 7 wrong answers out of 50)

If you scored in this range you are that percentage away from being a slave. Congratulations. Happy Day. You are well on your way to freedom, your head is right and you set a good example of what it looks like to be free. You are an excellent role model, and others around you may think you are a little militant, but they are secretly impressed at your bold fearless behavior. We need more Black people like you because you definitely know the difference between slavery and freedom, and whenever challenged, you choose freedom. Keep up the spirit of freedom and your future generations are destined to know the true meaning and practice of Freedom, Justice and Equality. You have your post-traumatic stress under control and do not allow it to overly influence or impact on your daily decisions to be free.

<u>GRADES 68 to 84</u>
(up to 16 wrong answers out of 50)

You're not completely sure yet whether or not being free is better than being a slave. You vascilate daily between both roles never really sure which side is most beneficial. By sheer will you are courageous enough to venture into freedom territory periodically, sometimes becoming overwhelmed and darting back into your perceived safety-net of being a slave. You can appear moderate in your views, often shielding how you really feel for fear of losing something. As your confidence in being free grows, you will look back upon your slave behavior as outrageous and unnecessary to your survival. Work to develop surefootedness by being around free Blacks, stop spending so much time with slaves who are comfortable and satisfied with their status. Your post-traumatic stress comes and goes frequently.

GRADES of 66 or less
(17 or more wrong answers out of 50)

Sorry. You, my friend, are straight out of 'ROOTS' a recognizable, hardcore slave, who doesn't even pretend to be free. You are dedicated to the principles, habits and ideas that our ancestors suffered from in bondage, and you have learned to justify your ancient attitudes and have rationalized that other Blacks yearning to be free are actually just ungrateful troublemakers trying to mess things up for everybody else. You are completely satisfied with your make-believe life ungrounded in any reality of our real condition. You may pretend to be cultural but actually you are trapped in the lowest dungeon of post-traumatic stress. Join up with an Afrocentric group, read history books and perhaps get in a support group to deal with your fears. They can be overcome but not until you admit that you have them. You are stuck in a time-warp and refuse to budge out of it. You may even think you are advanced far beyond other Black people who appear to you to be still dealing with issues that faded long ago. Take another look, poor soul. You, too can be free, but as for now you are a slave, and your chains are clearly visible to the trained eye of Blacks who are free. You need professional help like psychotherapy to raise your consciousness. No matter how hard you try you can never be white, and no matter how much you love them, you will never gain the acceptance you so desire.

Stop living in a pretend world. No matter how hard you try, you will never be white or fully accepted by white. Learn about yourself so you can learn to love yourself. The word "Self" means all of us as a Black people, a tribe who were stolen from our homeland and turned into the self-hating fools you see today.

There is salvation for you.

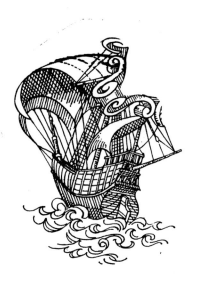

We have several current examples of our nearly collective slave-mentality. Back in April 2015 there were civil disruptions by community members who were protesting against the murder of young Black man who was murdered under suspicious circumstances by the Baltimore Police. There was the usual looting, rock and can throwing, yelling, cursing at the police that was touched off by our fearless youth. They are a generation who have been raised thinking that they need "things" in order to be whole. So they logically broke into certain businesses and took as much "stuff" as they could carry. Of course the media, especially CNN, exaggerated the situation. The protesters were charged with setting several businesses on fire including a CVS and a Senior Citizen Building. However, just as in Ferguson; it is entirely possible that "outside agitators" and "Provocateurs" started the fires, burned the cars and even threw some of the bricks at the police. We don't know who set those fires which was blamed on the youth protesters. They were called "thugs" and "criminals" by political leaders and local citizens. Over 5000 national guardsmen and other police were brought in to defend the city. The purpose of the protest got lost in the shuffle by the media and the people who started the problem stepped in claiming they wanted peace. At the printing of this book a Black female State Prosecutor has charged the 6 officers involved (3 white and 3 Black) with various levels of murder. The Black female Mayor is struggling to keep the enemy from using divide and conquer techniques to further splinter the city. The enemy's system of a Grand Jury review nearly guarantees the accused will be found NOT-GUILTY! The Slaves lose again.

MULTIPLE CHOICE QUIZ
FOR REINFORCEMENT

(To see if you remember what you should
have learned from the test answers)

MULTIPLE CHOICE QUIZ
FOR REINFORCEMENT

(These questions are based on the Freedom I.Q. Test)

1) African Americans and the American political system
   A___ are not compatible for progress.
   B___ work together.
   C___ Is our ace in the hole.

2) If I had to leave America, I would not want to live in
   A___ Paris.
   B___ Japan.
   C___ Africa.

3) There is no need for us to continue to
   C___ march.
   B___ complain.
   A___ laugh at white folks' jokes.

4) To protect myself I must remember to carry
   A___ a weapon.
   B___ Knowledge of the enemy.
   C___ proof of identity.

5) Our Black christian preachers continue to
   A___ Mislead us.
   B___ promote slavery.
   C___ pray for divine intervention.

6) A major problem of communication between
us is because of
A___ joblessness.
B_✓_ lying.
C___ stuttering.

7) Several tribes of Native-Americans used to be
A___ land owners.
B___ explorers.
C_✓_ slave owners.

8) Most police believe that "law" is to protect whites,
and "order" is
A___ Whatever they say.
B_✓_ something to keep Blacks in.
C___ a civil right.

9) We should take advantage of every aspect of
Freedom of Speech so
A___ we can talk freely.
B___ honesty will prevail.
C_✓_ we can trust.

10) We do not have enough emotional self-control
to own
A___ Cadillacs.
B_✓_ guns.
C___ property.

112

11) We need to stop having long drawn out miserable
    A___ birthday parties.
    B___ divorces.
    C___ funerals.

12) A lot of our pain is emotional and can be
    considered as
    A___ psychosomatic.
    B___ body memories.
    C___ low pain tolerance.

13) It makes no sense to sit around and wait on
    A___ reparations.
    B___ the bus.
    C___ a chance to sue somebody.

14) Calling and getting real help or assistance
    from Police is
    A___ undependable.
    B___ a form of security.
    C___ Fading.

15) Sports is the one universal activity that
    A___ entertains us.
    B___ wastes our time.
    C___ Makes white men rich.

16) We are just naturally funny and we can't help it if
    A___ we laugh at each other.
    B___ we act a fool.
    C___ Make jokes to hide our shame.

17) Dancing is not only beautiful and a form of exercise, it is

A___ a way to loosen up.

B___ an expression of hostility.

C___ cool.

18) We are a sexy, feeling people but we have a problem showing

A___ off in front of others.

B___ we are erotic.

C___ Sincere Affection.

19) If we have a choice, we will try anything possible to

A___ get home on time.

B___ get out of working.

C___ get to a party.

20) Parenting is not a natural science, we need instructions on

A___ Mothering and Fathering

B___ making formula.

C___ selecting a babysitter.

21) We should stop basing our diets and meal planning on

A___ supermarket prices.

B___ taste.

C___ our slave diet.

22) If we would stop being so uptight we would not suffer so much from

A___ loneliness.

B___ mistakes.

C___ constipation.

23) We have a slight fetish for good shoes that keeps us from having to
   A)___ wear the same pair.
   B)_✓_ walk barefoot.
   C)___ see a podiatrist.

24) We should stop giving our children books which focus on
   A)_✓_ Caucasian values.
   B)___ the occult.
   C)___ dead heroes.

25) We need new definitions and studies to interpret
   A)___ Swahili.
   B)___ "body language."
   C)_✓_ the metric system.

26) It's hard to imagine, but there are ways to discipline other than
   A)___ abandonment.
   B)_✓_ whipping.
   C)___ fussing.

27) Although beneficial, the one thing we will never have between us is
   A)_✓_ honesty.
   B)___ a garden.
   C)___ mass unity.

28) One source of confusion in our children is what goes on in
   A)_✓_ the home.
   B)___ Day Care Centers.
   C)___ NAACP meetings.

29) Many Black men get in trouble with their
    women for
    A)___ being overweight.
    B)_✓ being outside too much.
    C)___ not bathing.

30) The one item that overwhelms us and creates a
    lot of arguments is
    A)___ Cable T.V.
    B)___ overtime work.
    C)_✓ how we spent our money.

31) The one time we really show unity with each
    other is at
    A)___ Family Reunions.
    B)_✓ Sunday church service.   ▷
    C)___ concerts.

32) More than any other medical ailment, we are
    more predisposed to have
    A)_✓ depression.
    B)_✓ hypertension.
    C)___ corns.

33) Bland may be fine for some, but we like our foods
    spiked with
    A)___ fat back.
    B)___ wheat germ.
    C)_✓ hot sauce.

34) The one responsibility Black males have yet to
    conquer is
    A)_✓ holding a job.
    B)___ fatherhood.
    C)___ reckless driving.

35) Often we don't eat right and worry too much and end up having
   A)___ no friends.
   B)___ obesity.
   C)_/_ Heart Disease.

36) Even if we integrate socially, we should never
   A)_/_ try to be white.
   B)___ marry whites.
   C)___ be proud of it.

37) We should start standing behind people we believe in and stop
   A)___ criticizing.
   B)_/_ being disloyal.
   C)___ Constantly disagreeing.

38) It is impossible to worship God without a church, temple or
   A)_/_ congregation.
   B)___ Bible.
   C)___ tent revival.

39) We need to reorganize our time so there is no special value for
   A)_/_ Monday night football.
   B)___ weekends.
   C)___ lunch.

40) There should be special workplace orientation for
   A)_/_ unskilled laborers.
   B)___ Black supervisors.
   C)___ alcoholics.

41) We place too much emphasis on trying to impress others with our
   A)__ marriage ceremony.
   B)__ diamond size.
   C)__ celebrity contacts.

42) Since it doesn't help, our people should stop
   A)__ Tithing.
   B)__ rioting.
   C)__ petitioning the government.

43) Worshipping God is a personal activity and need not be
   A)__ integrated.
   B)__ all day long.
   C)__ based on mystery.

44) Our children must learn to express their ideas and feelings so
   A)__ they can relate.
   B)__ they aren't stifled.
   C)__ others can hear.

45) We have no resources to escape America so we remain
   A)__ hostages.
   B)__ indoors.
   C)__ dissatisfied.

46) The projects and ghettoes across America promote
   A)__ selling drugs.
   B)__ claustrophobia.
   C)__ roaches.

47) We need to re-educate in some of our basic
behaviors and
A)___ habits.
B)__/ shopping.
C)___ saving the earth.

48) Our entire genetic memory is contained in our
skin in the form of
A)___ pores.
B)__ Melanin.
C)___ scar tissue.

49) We are not qualified to go forth in the future until
we understand
A)___ mathematics.
B)__ the past.
C)___ the tax laws.

50) Due to our post-traumatic stress disorder we are
unable to decide on
A)__ the best plan for us.
B)___ good white people.
C)___ stock choices.

THIS IS THE END OF THE
MULTIPLE CHOICE QUIZ

ANSWER SHEET FOR MULTIPLE CHOICE
REINFORCEMENT QUIZ

1 – A	26 – B
2 – C	27 – C
3 – C	28 – B
4 – B	29 – B
5 – B	30 – C
6 – B	31 – A
7 – C	32 – B
8 – B	33 – C
9 – B	34 – B
10 – B	35 – C
11 – C	36 – B
12 – B	37 – B
13 – A	38 – C
14 – A	39 – B
15 – C	40 – B
16 – B	41 – A
17 – B	42 – B
18 – C	43 – A
19 – B	44 – B
20 – A	45 – A
21 – B	46 – B
22 – C	47 – A
23 – B	48 – B
24 – A	49 – B
25 – B	50 – B

SCORE SHEET FOR MULTIPLE CHOICE
REINFORCEMENT QUIZ

1) The top score possible is 100. (2 points for each question)

2) Subtract 2 points for each wrong answer.

3) Write your score here ⬜ This is your grade.

4) Interpretation of your score is on page 105.

This score should be higher than your grade on the Freedom I.Q.

**THIS SECTION PROVIDES FURTHER
INFORMATION TO HELP YOU
DESLAVE YOURSELF**

* Please be advised that the following pages are only intended to lightly touch upon medical and psychological topics deemed relative to a diagnosis of Post-Traumatic Stress. It is by no means complete or detailed in its explanations. However, the principles referred to are easily understood and recognizable by almost any layman. It is suggested, as always, that you embark upon your own research and apply the information in this book to your own conclusions.

Please view copies of Hidden Colors 1, 2 and 3 produced and conceived by Tariq Nasheed so you can further your education about self.

POST TRAUMATIC STRESS GENETICALLY INHERITED FROM OUR SLAVE HISTORY

Post-traumatic Stress Disorder, as defined in the Diagnostic and Statistical Manual of Mental Disorders, Third Edition (DSM-III), Washington, D.C., American Psychiatric Association, says, "The essential feature is the development of characteristic symptoms after the experiencing of a psychologically traumatic event or events outside of the range of human experience usually considered to be normal. The characteristic symptoms involve re-experiencing the traumatic event, numbing of responsiveness to, or involvement with, the external world, and a variety of other autonomic, dysphoric, or cognitive symptoms."

autonomic means: Under the control of the nervous system, self-driven.
dysphoric means: State of dissatisfaction, anxiety, restlessness.
cognitive means: Mental process of perception.

This definition was modified in DSM-III-R in 1987 to cover those events that are "outside of the range of usual human experience and that would be markedly distressing to almost anyone."

Post-traumatic Stress Disorder (PTSD) or Post-traumatic Syndrome, gained popularity following the emotional complaints from the Vietnam veterans of the 1970's, and at that time was referred to as "post-Vietnam syndrome." It was acknowledged as a real disorder in 1980 by the Veterans Administration. Previously it had been considered as a cause of the dismay suffered by the survivors of World War I, and included in this category were the survivors of Hitler's disasterous regime thereafter called "Concentration Camp Syndrome." An invaluable medical text titled "The Neuroses" which discusses such post-traumatic stress, says of the concentration camp,

"Those millions confined to concentration camps were exposed to differing kinds of stress. The threat of imminent death or permanent incarceration was suffered by all. The intensity of the threats was variable. Those exposed to the open brutalities and killings and executions of other prisoners and who were required to participate in prison camp persecutions and burials, while surviving separation from family members and friends, suffered differently from others incarcerated and deprived physically owing to severe shortages of food, clothing, housing, activity, and opportunities for needed human contact, emotional support, and stimulation. The vast marjority of those survivors who had symptoms impairing their personality functioning experienced the full range of terrifying and despair-creating stresses: personal assaults of all kinds, perception of brutality and killings of others, desecration of bodies, separation from families and friends, and physical illness and deprivations. Many became 'living corpses' in the concentration camp." The survivors were diagnosed as having acute, chronic and delayed post-traumatic stress disorders. It is said they lived (live) in a "continual state of dread of recurrent of the event, as well as fear that it will happen again." Doctors have isolated several basic response reactions from older Vets of World War I, Vietnam and Concentration Camps:
1) Death imprint
2) Death anxiety
3) Psychic numbing
4) Impaired human relations
5) The meaning of disaster

Restlessness, tension and chronic anxiety with inability to forget or put aside memories of the stresses they endured often lead these survivors to isolate themselves from family and all social life. Acute and Post-traumatic Stress Syndrome occurs after severe physical and/or emotional trauma such as what our ancestors experienced during slavery. This trauma commenced around 1555 and we are still suffering, stunned and practically immobile today as a result of it. There are two types of post-traumatic states; one with immediate reaction, and one with delayed onset. We experience delayed onset manifested by our feelings of inadequacy, intense fear, self-hatred, feelings of helplessness, loss of control and perceived threats of annihilation. Post-traumatic Stress Syndrome can be experienced by one individual after a traumatic event, or by large groups of people who shared a trauma by way of inheritability. This conclusion is based on more detailed study into the psychodynamics of Post-traumatic Stress which include self-defeating behavior, guilt, depression, loss of personal relationships, no sense of personal identity, and disassociation and depersonalization with others of ones own kind. The above is a complete definition of our current condition inclusive. Understanding and accepting this definition is complicated by the fact that most of us think that the above description applies only to other Black people – and not ourselves. We readily agree "that's how 'they' are," when in effect, that's how "we" are. Some of us have managed to mask our symptoms better than others due to education and finances. It is suggested that we do further investigation into Post-traumatic Stress Syndrome and learn more about this type of public health problem which fits our condition. Slavery was an emotional catastrophe for us, a catastrophe perceived only by us that remains unsettled.

GENETIC FACTORS CONTRIBUTING
TO OUR DELAYED STRESS

A variety of psychological, physical and genetic factors impact on our daily behavior in and out of the home. This genetic underpinning has often been ignored or disregarded as having any validity since we are removed over 400 years from slavery. Plus, we don't know, and have never known any slaves, and we are so free today. But certain genetic based emotions remain with us now which is why we still mention and can't forget about slavery. Not only can we not forget it, but we rarely allow anybody else to forget it either. Although we have not made the kind of educational, social or economic progress we hope for, our living conditions today, even some of our worst, are still 100% better than how we lived during slavery. This is why members of other races don't know what we keep harping about. Our dissatisfaction about slavery is practically self-propelled – it's in the blood. The blood of our ancestors which flows strongly through our veins, pumping in our hearts and drumming in our pulse, pulls on us in a way that is medically undetected but deeply rooted in our being. Ideas of dormant dissatisfaction as an inherited transmission is delivered from generation to generation, and we have no real control over it. Even those of us who pretend through self-hypnosis that our slave history is unimportant today, let bygones by bygones and what's done is done. If we sit very still in a quiet place and concentrate we can hear the wailing cries, the clang of the shackles, and the pop of the whip. Our indepth knowledge and understanding of what our ancestors endured has a substantial genetic basis, a connection resembling a 400 year long chain. We feel their grief and become saddened and then angry. This anger must be confronted in ourselves and understood. And we must begin the grieving process which we have never done.

SURVIVING ABUSE AND TORTURE

Investigating the long term effect of torture is another aspect of this study on whether or not we are still slaves. Our honored ancestors were stronger in will during slavery than we are in mental capacity after being freed. The physical energy they shared is unprecedented. Today we are too fearful of damaging our ego with failure. We can compare our durability today with what our ancestors outlived over 100 years ago.

Forms of Torture our Ancestors Endured:
Verbal abuse
Beating
Blindfolding
Forced standing
Threats
Prevention of personal hygiene
Being pulled by the hair
Witnessing torture
Being stripped naked
Prevention of urination/defecation
Isolation
Sleep Deprivation
Restriction of movement
Beating on the soles of the feet
No medical care
Exposure to extreme heat and cold
Rape (Women and men)

Denial of privacy
Punishment of family
Vermin-infested surroundings
Food deprivation
Hanging by wrists
Not enough water
Cold showers
Blows on the ears
Carrying of weights
Fondling of genitals
Asphyxiation
Submersion in water
Exposure to bright light
Excrement in food
Burning
Rope bondage
Stretching of extremeties
Castration
Separation from family

When we read the above list and realize that our ancestors survived most of the hardships noted, how dare we, with all the conveniences we have at our disposal today, claim that we are unable to do something. Our enslaved ancestors hung on to what they knew for as long as they could, by the mid-1600's most had forgotten about freedom and being independent. They adapted to survive. Each ensuing generation became further and further removed from freedom and independence in the true sense of the word. Thus commenced the start of our present relationship with whites, one where they are the providers/givers and we are the recipients/beggars. It's an increasingly unhealthy relationship wherein both parties are unhappy with the arrangement but don't know how to get out of it comfortably or honorably. We have more education, resources, contacts, mobility, communication, energy and transportation then any of our ancestors ever dreamed of having, yet we have produced less with more than they ever did. New information and research is constantly being unveiled about hundreds of tools, equipment, contraptions and systems we designed and made. We have learned about schools, colleges, institutions and entrepreneurial enterprises built by Black men and Black women since post-slavery that rival any modern accomplishment today. We forfeited these achievements when we traded self-determination and self-reliance for social integration thirty years ago. So today the playing field is so lopsided with every other nationality in America making progress in every aspect of life except us. We lag behind but we have always lagged behind but managed to muster up enough gumption to do what was necessary to survive against the worst odds possible. It is critical now for us to work to stop being a slave. A slave to laziness, a slave to disunity, a slave to material gains, a slave to our low desires, a slave to false pride, a slave to face value and vice.

Our purpose in life cannot continue to be work-eat-sleep and pay rent. This is not saying that food, clothes and shelter are not paramount. We must stop looking at whites and comparing ourselves with them as if they are our competition. We can only compete with ourselves, or others just like us. We have nothing to be embarrassed or ashamed about. We can make voluntary sacrifices now to plan sanely for our futures, or we will shortly be forced to make involuntary sacrifices due to the conditions prevailing around us. It is a strange people who refuse to take instruction to better themselves. And it is a lazy people who would rather beg than build. Education and scholarship are not our greatest priority, our greatest need is a re-education in instinct, feelings, habits and the will. We have to be de-slaved.

THE EFFECT OF BEING TAKEN HOSTAGE

Our ancestors were taken as hostage. Analysts say the majority of individuals taken hostage never fully recover from the experience and that the emotional impact is long term. The shock of being kidnapped cuts one off from the outside world they are familiar with, they lose track of time, place and purpose and become disoriented. L.B. Taylor, Jr., author of "Hostage," a book about kidnapping and terrorism as a global threat says, "in many hostage incidents the victims initially think only of escape or survival, but after days or weeks of close contact with their captors, their feelings can turn to fondness and understanding. Psychiatrists content that this is actually a return to infancy, when a baby depends upon everything from others. Thus, when hostages find themselves totally dependent upon other persons for survival, they revert to rather infantile behavior. They come to identify with their captors and often even sympathize with them. Conversely, they develop a certain degree of hostility towards the authorities who are trying to gain their release."

Charles Figley, director of the Traumatic Stress Research Program at Purdue University in Indiana says, "most mental health officials recommend a 'decompression period' for hostages immediately after release..." The American Psychiatric Association Task Force on Terrorism agrees. Both of the above quotes from authorities on the topic of hostages and hostage release provide a rational explanation as to part of what has happened to us, except we had no 'decompression period' or debriefing process awaiting us after our ancestors were released from physical slavery. But if the above trend of human behavior is accurate, we can certainly understand how our ultra-dependency makes us continue to believe and plead for justice from the descendants of the slave masters who look exactly like them. Yes, we are dependent. But we fail to understand the critical aspects of our absolute total dependency on others for survival. Let us look at this pattern of dependency.

Our ancestors were dependent based on being dominated by the slave masters who subjected them to brutality that was convincing. Since they were prevented from involvement in plans, decisions and control of issues providing food, clothing or shelter ... they grew to accept their dependency as somewhat rewarding. If the master didn't provide it, they didn't get it. The slaves believed that the master would always provide for them because he owned them – they were his. He was vicariously responsible for them. Today our dependency has expanded. The benefits are better, bigger and quicker; they just don't last long enough. And today we have more faith in the politics of negotiation. We continue to believe that eventually we will get our just due, and grasp our share of what our ancestors worked for. It remains, to us, an unpaid debt, even if they were forced to do the work, they did it. We feel that as a result of their involuntary contributions, that we have a stake in America – the slave provided the brawn and the master provided the brains. Which brings us to right now. Since becoming free we no longer have to wait until our former slave masters decide to give us something, now we have permission to walk right straight up to the door and ask for what we want. No, we don't get every thing that we ask for, but we do get more than we are denied. It's a slow arduous process but things are coming along. Just like our ancestors, we have grown to see our dependency as rewarding – just not enough.

There is a political rumor in Washington spreading across the country, already in document form, that the welfare/food stamp/medicaid system as we know it, is about to change. Several suggestions are being made regarding how to move us from the welfare system and provoke us to become a working class citizen. Others of us are suffering from the backlash of a wounded economy where no work is available, and unemployment, disability and veterans benefits have run out for millions of us already. The plantation is breaking down and we are being turned out and turned away on several fronts. We are in trouble.

There is only one precedent for such action. That precedent took place at the end of the Civil War when hordes of slaves were dismissed from plantations. Not all of the slaves wanted to be free. They didn't know what freedom or self-responsibility meant, because for almost four centuries they had been totally dependent upon the slave master. Some of the slaves are recorded to have begged their masters to let them stay, to allow them to work on for room and board. Many did stay – for as long as they could, willing to accept further debasement to avoid that foggy and fuzzy thing called "freedom."

Freedom has been taught, defined and demonstrated by example. It is impossible to live in a multi-cultural society and be independent, but what we can have is equality, co-dependency. Right now we are at everyone's mercy, no one is at ours. So even if the government is going to abandon us it is, presumed by us, to be a permanent responsibility – taking care of us. The government cannot afford to, and are no longer willing to, bankroll our inabilities. They are slowly closing the barn doors on us. While we stomp around outside mumbling our discontent. Losing one's freedom by force is one thing, but rejecting freedom by choice is another. Our slave history and our current behavior have become transposed, reversed and no one knows the difference.

IS GENOCIDE STILL BEING PRACTICED ON US DESCENDANTS OF SLAVES?

According to Article II of the United Nations Convention on the Prevention and Punishment of the Crime of Genocide (adopted 12/9/48), they list the following as "Acts of Genocide":

A) Killing members of the group – Manifests for us by police brutality, front line in wars, illegal medical experimentation, AIDS and lynchings by rumor and blackballing.

B) Causing serious bodily harm to members of the group – (See Above).

C) Deliberately inflicting on the group conditions of life calculated to bring about its physical destruction in whole or in part – Manifests for us as drugs in our communities, guns, red-lining, inadequate education, discrimination and welfare.

D) Imposing measures intended to prevent births within the group – Manifests for us as experimental birth control, ready abortions, and women's lib teachings.

E) <u>Forcibly transferring children of the group to another group</u> — Manifests for us as busing, interracial adoptions, and transracial foster home placement.

By now we should all be able to define the above headings and outline the hostage situation our slave ancestors were in for 400 years. These are modern times and most of us think of genocide as a foreign term usually reserved for some far off place in the East, practiced by political radicals or religious zealots. We are not accustomed to considering genocide as a slow staggered process spread thinly but consistently for decade after decade insidiously.

<u>JEWELRY STYLES INHERITED FROM SLAVERY</u>
(Made of gold, silver or metals)

>   Chain necklaces (especially rope)
>   Chain bracelets
>   Ankle chains
>   Wide band watches
>   Purses with chain straps
>   Clothes with chain designs (vests/jackets/dresses)
>   Chain link belts

NOTE:
We did not wear precious metals or iron in the 15th century as jewelry in Africa. The majority of those captured were from jungle tribes specializing in agriculture, hunting, intricate legal structures, wars with neighboring tribes, home building, rituals and boating. Gold did not have the same value to the natives as it had

to the European sailors who manned the slave ships. The Blacks who were captured or tricked into slavery were not always from progressive societies like those existing in Egypt or elsewhere along the North-eastern areas of Africa. "Chains" and wrist ankle irons made an indelible imprint upon our psyches and as times became more modernized, designers (Black and white) used precious metals such as gold and silver to camouflage the original uses of these items. Chain jewelry is symbolic of the chains our ancestors wore during slavery, and we are attracted to these kinds of symbols because of our memory of them. However, we think that we just like them because of their fashion value or because they are a usable way to own gold or silver. In other places in Africa the people used chains for tools and in building. The white race is the only race who used them for bondage. So even if they can no longer force us to wear chains, we are so programmed that we pick them out and choose to wear them on our own.

CULINARY DELIGHTS INHERITED
FROM SLAVERY

1) Chittlins and hog maws
2) Greens and corn bread
3) Red beans and rice
4) Blackeyed peas and candy yams
   (and lima beans)
5) Grits
   AND
6) FRIED CHICKEN

Historically, there is nowhere on the African continent where "fried chicken" was a part of the menu. Most of us think we like fried chicken because it is relatively inexpensive, fairly easy to prepare and available in practically every store or restaurant. During slavery our ancestors considered getting a whiff of chicken frying in hot grease as close to heaven as possible for their olfactory senses. And of course getting to actually eat one of those crispy crusty flour sprinkled hot juicy pieces of fried chicken was indeed a delicacy. It was also an acquired taste that represented such a treat to us that we continued throughout the years to select and eat it. Possibly our great attraction to fried chicken is that it satisfies us in a way no other meat is capable of doing. We may be experiencing a repeat of the thrill our ancestors experienced when they got their hands on some fried chicken which was 100 percent better than the poor vittles they usually had to eat. Most of us already know that our slave ancestors learned to eat pork, the worst parts of the pig, because the slave master gave them the pig's intestines, bowel sack, liver, heart, brains and tails, ears, hooves and heads after hog-killing season – a special treat. Some of us still consider it a special treat. We buy and eat more fried chicken than any other meat in our areas.

WHAT OUR SLAVE ANCESTORS WANTED FROM THE SLAVEMASTER – in 1555

1) Fair pay for their labor
2) Better housing
3) Proper access to medical care
4) Education for their education
5) A safe, fear-free environment to live in
6) Protection from brutality
7) Opportunity to work
8) Protection for their women and children
9) Political representation
10) An end to subjection

WHAT AFRICAN-AMERICANS WANT FROM THE GOVERNMENT TODAY – in 1994

1) A job
2) Better housing
3) Proper access to medical care
4) Education for our children
5) A safe, fear-free environment to live in
6) Protection from police brutality
7) Equal opportunity in the workplace
8) Protection for our women and children
9) Political representation
10) An end to racism

Of course today we also want recognition and an apology, or some kind of sign that whites are just as concerned about our condition as they are about their own. Our ancestors died disappointed. So do we. There is obviously something wrong with our approach to acquiring these natural rights deserved by all civilized humanity.

THE BILL OF RIGHTS

(From the United States Constitution)

The first 10 amendments to the Constitution were ratified December 15, 1791.

AMENDMENT 1
<u>Congress shall make no law</u> respecting the establishment of religion, or prohibiting the free exercise thereof; or abridging the freedom of speech, or of the press; or the right of the people peaceably to assemble, and to petition the Government for redress and grievances.

AMENDMENT 2
<u>A well regulated Militia</u>, being necessary to the security of a free State, the right of the people to keep and bear Arms, shall not be infringed.

AMENDMENT 3
<u>No Soldier shall</u>, in time of peace be quartered in any house, without the consent of the Owner, nor in time of war, but in a manner to be prescribed by law.

AMENDMENT 4
<u>The right of the people</u> to be secure in their persons, houses, papers, and effects, against unreasonable searches and seizures, shall not be violated, and no Warrants shall issue, but upon probable cause, supported by Oath or affirmation, and particularly describing the place to be searched, and the persons or things to be seized.

AMENDMENT 5

No person shall be held to answer for a capital, or otherwise infamous crime, unless on a presentment or indictment of a Grand Jury, except in cases arising in the land or naval forces, or in the Militia, when in actual service in time of War or public danger; nor shall any person be subject for the same offense to be twice put in jeopardy of life or limb; nor shall be compelled in any criminal case to be a witness against himself, nor be deprived of life, liberty, or property, without due process of law; nor shall private property be taken for public use, without just compensation.

AMENDMENT 6

In all criminal prosecutions, the accused shall enjoy the right to a speedy and public trial, by an impartial jury of the State and district wherein the crime shall have been committed, which district shall have been previously ascertained by law, and to be informed of the nature and cause of the accusation; to be confronted with the witnesses against him; to have compulsory process for obtaining witnesses in his favor, and to have the Assistance of Counsel for his defense.

AMENDMENT 7

In Suits at common law, here the value in controversy shall exceed twenty dollars, the right of trial by jury shall be preserved, and no fact tried by a jury, shall be otherwise re-examined in any Court of the United States, than according to the rules of the common law.

AMENDMENT 8

Excessive bail shall not be required, nor excessive fines imposed, nor cruel and unusual punishments inflicted.

AMENDMENT 9

The enumeration in the Constitution, of certain rights, shall not be construed to deny or disparage others retained by the people.

AMENDMENT 10

The powers not delegated to the United States by the Constitution, nor prohibited by it to the States, are reserved to the States respectively, or to the people.

The above 10 rules of the Bill of Rights are presented to allow us an opportunity to examine the rights and benefits allegedly accorded to each and every American, those born within the boundaries of the U.S.A. – or – those who take up citizenship here. The only Amendment which we have exercised is number 1. We have explored and utilized every aspect of Amendment #1 – mainly denoting; freedom of religion, freedom of speech, freedom of press, freedom to assemble (such as in marches), and freedom to 'petition the Government for a redress of grievances.' We have partaken in all of the above "rights" and "freedoms" with only slight success when aligned with the actual list of complaints we have about being denied our "rights." We have become stagnated in Amendment #1 because these "rights" do not require much more than talk – Freedom of Speech, belief – Freedom of Religion, marching – Freedom to Assemble, and begging – Freedom to Petition the Government..., the other 9 Amendments have not received much attention by us, and we generally believe they are not as important as Amendment #1, providing overall 'freedom of expression.' Expression is creativity. And we pride ourselves on being a creative people. We are. But, it seems that since our ancestors were denied the very basic freedoms outlined in the First Amendment, that by the time we as their descendents acquired them, we are overjoyed. Ecstatic, to finally be able to speak aloud our ideas, worship as we please, organize protests and make demands of the government. Participating in the varied aspects of the First Amendment has taken up a lot of our time and attention. We have built huge conglomerates around utilization each "right" allowed, and have long documented histories and heroes who excelled in those categories. Our ancestors had been stifled so long and crushed under the boundaries and restrictions of slavery that when finally permitted to be themselves, they found that the only self they knew how to be was a physically free slave. Carrying the scars and disfigurements of slavery in our heads, with all our natural habits and security beliefs dismantled; has left us with confused values, hypocrisy and anxiety . . . still a slave. So beyond the First Amendment, opportunities, provisions, compliments and invitations from others, possibly trying to help us, fall on deaf ears. We are unable to be positive about potential because of our inferiority complex rooted in our slave history. Positive thinking only works with a sturdy foundation of high self-esteem. Our self-esteem is blocked from blooming because of the embarassment, regret and worry. Of course in order to be politically correct today, many of us when found in an integrated environment, acknowledge in cooperative tones: "slavery is over," and "that was then, this is now," or "we have to move on," or "we should all just respect each other," or "that's all over with." In psychiatry these statements would be considered "self-talk" or a type of biofeedback to repress pain and shield ourselves from scrutiny. Whites are no doubt somewhat confused about our affable forgiving nature. They can't imagine how any intelligent person could claim to forget something that devastated our people like slavery did and continues to impact. Another area given little attention is that slavery ended almost abruptly, (physical bondage), and there was no special recognition, no "40 Acres and a Mule," and no improvement of condition or apology. No apology has ever come, and will never come. Yet many of us still expect one. The closest thing to an apology we have received is the bestowance of the rights/privileges in the First Amendment. Talk, pray, march and beg. That is how we have defined the benefits of the First Amendment in the Bill of Rights. The Constitution should be examined in the same way to see if we really understand it. But the Bill of Rights opened new avenues for us, we just don't know which street to take. Until we claim self-worth, internal peace and truth; if the civilization lasts, we will either be in the same condition in 20 years, or worse.

Although it may be hard to imagine things getting worse, a wise prophet said, "The Worst is Yet to Come." And for us it keeps coming every day. We are essentially blocked from progress by the very things we hold dear.

1) European religions
2) A job
3) Politics

European religions hold us back because the christian based religions we believe in contain all of the principles, reasons and instructions to keep us enslaved emotionally, mentally and physically. All forms of European religions we practice must be included in this category. It is shocking, it is insulting and it is unreasonable – but it must be done. The main option that would help free us is to give up our belief and practice of each and every religion that we inherited or have adopted that was authored by European, Anglo-Saxon, Caucasians. This is not to insult any Caucasian and the christian religion of their fathers. And they have every righteous right to believe and practice them. But we must admit, their belief in christianity has netted them much better gains than our belief in it has. But because we do not understand the power of suggestion and the power of absolute belief, we don't realize the subliminal messages and soul pulling weight of their Holy Bible. Because most of us don't want to be Godless, as spiritual as we are; we are terrified at the thought of trying to exist without that religion to dictate to us and comfort us.

Christianity is the only tie that binds us to our current condition. If we were to choose anything else, it would require a complete turnaround in our lives that would be disruptive and long lasting. This is why we fear to give up our European religions. This "fear" is what was used to teach it to our slave ancestors and burn it into their hearts. The information here is not to be applied just to those of us who attend church, believe or run one. The teachings of this European religion are far reaching, even into those who do not attend church, but who know about it. This group encompasses all of us. We have all been exposed to the teachings of Christianity. Sometimes the very worst, lewd or foulest member of our nationality can be found wearing a cross. Our Black entertainers, athletes, teachers, doctors, lawyers, bus drivers, street cleaners, rap artists, politicians, etc., etc., etc. – ALL HAVE, OR OWN A CROSS. Maybe a necklace, maybe a wall plaque, maybe a ring, but we are all diluted with the symbols and teachings of this religion which was provided to us by our ancestors and kept them enslaved. It is said that the slave masters gave our ancestors only certain segments of the bible at first. Then when they were sure we completely understood and believed that part, they gave us the other passages, because they knew we were so absorbed with religion that we would hold steadfast to it forever. The first parts of the bible they gave us highlighted the areas where certain verses implied that Blacks should enjoy slavery, and being a slave is what God had chosen for them as a life. So by the time the slaves got to the latter parts of the bible prohibiting servitude they already deeply believed the former. This is simple psychology. You cannot stop being a slave until you give up slavery's benchmark – the religion of christianity. This may cause panic in many of us.

A JOB – while many of us are able to trace certain roots of our problems to the discrimination practiced against Black men over the decades, which prevents him from securing work and getting money to support his family; there are some things going on with us that a job simply will not solve. There are tenents we have to learn about work that preceed any requirement we may have about the importance of a job. There is new education needed regarding the work ethic. The purpose of work is not just to make money to survive, it ought to be more firmly planted than that. Work is what ties a man to the earth, makes him feel like he belongs and makes him feel powerful and satisfied. A regular job does not stimulate these values even when latched to large sums of salary. And if you are working for someone else (you know who) and you do feel the above emotions, then you are a pureblooded absolute slave. Because the feelings mentioned above are reserved for those in ownership positions. Labor is an extremely important part of education that is routinely ignored. We are taught that the job is the work and the money we get form the job will make everything else okay. Money does not create enough motivation in us to go to work on a routine basis. We either like what we do, see it as a stepping stone or enjoy the title. Every negative reaction we have to work or being out of work is grounded in our slave history. Since becoming genetically impaired in the 15th century, we have had unhappy and unrealistic expectations about work. Work has never represented anything in our history except pain and drudgery, domination and exhaustion. So until we work out the remaining kinks we have about work, no job will ever satisfy us eternally. It doesn't matter whether or not the economy improves, unless we first change our idea about work it won't do any good.

POLITICS – or legislative government interaction, has not been good for us. Many of us have seen our politicians clean their act up, change their M.O. and conservatize their opinions so as to be accepted by the mass voters and incumbents. We have seen some fail, and we are seeing now many who succeed. While they speak rowdy and firm while on the campaign, once in we get to see them grow quiet and sullen, unable to penetrate such a firmly established institution anchored by white males. The "Right to Vote" is another long awaited for benefit. Many slaves were able to qualify for an in-house position, while other slaves were routinely appointed because of a need for human assistance. The other king-pin on the plantation was the carriage driver, the next was the black "slave driver." He, as previously mentioned, worked up under the white overseer. He in effect had a supervisory position directed by management, or can be, as we see today, a councilman, a mayor or a delegate of some sort. The slave driver could only exercise his authority within the guidelines of the overseer and the master, although he had been politically appointed because of his perfect qualifications. The slave driver's job was to drive the slaves in the different direction of work for the master. Our politician's job is to drive us in the direction of believing in the power of the vote, even though he has no proof of it. We think if we don't vote we won't be counted at all, or that we will lose our political voice on issues that affect us and our communities. The American government approved us for voting in about 1870 – Yipee! Since then we have voted by the millions, and so far none of our conditions have been permanently rectified. Our Black "Firsts" have not been followed by seconds, thirds or fourths. As we progressively run out of things to integrate, it will become increasingly clear that our so-called political gains are receding to never show their balloted face again. Politics means policy and until we are able to itemize the policies we deem most important, and lean all our energies towards that end, our politicians will remain in the slave driver tradition. All proponents of politics will argue these points.

CONCLUSIONS

Unless we do something about our religion, jobs and politics – plus our names, we will continue to be mired in slavery and abject unconditional servitude. Those of us who want to hold on to the practices and beliefs that keep us enslaved should be allowed to do so. And those of us who desire to be free cannot and will not be interrupted. Hopefully this test book will let each of us see ourselves and our condition crystal clear. There is much to be discussed.

The most important test question remains: are you still a slave?
Check every day.

GENERAL SLAVE PROFILE
(Post-traumatic Stress Disorders
Inherited from Slavery)

1. Refers to other Blacks as "you guys," instead of <u>Sister</u> or <u>Brother</u>.

2. Wears brand-name clothes so designer's name is clearly visible.

3. Wears a cross around the neck, on lapel or hanging on wall in home.

4. Refuses to call other Blacks by their African or Arabic names.

5. Enjoys integrated or all white bars, clubs or entertainment spots.

6. Buys Black children white dolls and books featuring white characters.

7. Consults the Holy Bible daily or weekly and defends christianity.

8. Hangs portraits of a white Jesus, the Last Supper or Crucifix in home.

9. Becomes happy and animated when talking to whites.

10. Delights in becoming, or admiring, those who attain a "Black First."

11. Congratulates Blacks who earn political appointments.

12. Is thrilled to participate in multicultural events.

13. Dyes hair blonde, wears blue or green contacts.

14. Uses skin lighteners on face and body in secret.

15. Has parties and invites Black and white guests.

16. Hangs the flag out on 4th of July, wears one on lapel or hat.

17. Believes the past is not important since it's over and done.

18. Buys cards and gifts to celebrate every European holiday.

19. Promotes their children to participate in integrated activities.

20. Attends an integrated church and is proud of it as progress.

21. Wears dreads, braids or African garb and has a white mate.

22. Has a best friend or confidant who is white.

23. Delights in moving into or living in an all-white neighborhood.

24. Sells illicit drugs to their own people.

25. Steals and rips off their own people with no remorse.

26. Persists in eating pork no matter what they know about it.

I want to leave you with one last clear picture.
Imagine this: What if all the white people in America
woke up tomorrow morning and all of the Black people
were gone? What would they do? Well. Their lives
would go on virtually unchanged. They might miss a
few friends, have to hire new workers on the job, or get
another laborer of some type. But for the most part, they
would still:

> use the telephone
> turn on the electric lights
> go to the supermarket
> cook on a gas stove
> ride the subway
> pay at the toll booth
> attend a movie
> travel on an airplane
> go to the hospital
> eat at McDonald's
> visit NASA
> cash their checks at the bank

etc. etc. White people would continue their existence
uninterrupted.

NOW – imagine this:

What if all the Black people in America woke up
tomorrow morning and all the white people were gone?
Pandemonium! Do you get it? The above is the clearest
example possible to demonstrate our 100% total dependency on others. We are not free. We are slaves.
Because FREE people do not have to deal with discrimination, segregation or racism – because FREE people
have equality. And we do not.

ABBREVIATED BIBLIOGRAPHY

History of the Negro People in America, 1619 to 1880, George W. Williams, G.P. Putnam's Sons, 1882

Light and Truth, Universal History of the Colored and the Indian Race, R.B. Lewis, Committee of Colored Gentlemen, 1836

History of Slavery and The Slave Trade, W.O. Blake, H. Miller Publishers, 1857

History of the Colored Race in America, Origin and Development of Slavery, William T. Alexander, A.M., Palmetto Publishers, 1897

Cotton is King and Pro-Slavery Arguments, E.N. Elliott, L.L.D. Pirtchard, Abbott & Loomis Publishers, 1860

Refugee: or Narratives of Fugitive Slaves in Canada, Benjamin Drew, John P. Jewett & Co., 1856

American Slavery and Finances, Hon. Robert J. Walker, M.A., William Ridgeway Press, 1864

New "Reign of Terror" in the Slaveholding States, American Anti-Slavery Society Publishers, 1860

Papers Relative to the Restriction of Slavery, King, Taylor & Talmadge, Hall & Atkinson Publishers, 1819

History of the Negro Race in America (1619 to 1800),
G.P. Putnam & Sons, 1883

American Slavery and Finances, London, 1864

*The American Slave Code in Theory and Practice: Its
Distinctive Features Shown By Its Statutes, Judi-
cial Decisions and Illustrative Facts*, William
Goodell, American and Foreign Anti-Slavery
Society, 1853

The History of Slavery and the Slave Trade, Ancient
and Modern, W.O. Blake, H. Miller, 1860

Slavery Ordained of God, Rev. Fred A. Ross, D.D.,
J.B. Lippincott & Co., 1859

*An Historical Sketch of Slavery from The Earliest
Periods*, Thomas R.R. Cobb, T. & J.W. Thompson
& Co., 1858

Narrative of an American Slave, James Williams, The
American Anti-Slavery Society, 1833

Facts for Baptist Churches, A.T. Foss and E.
Mathews, The American Baptist Free Mission
Society, 1850

Early Reflections and Life of Dr. James Still, J.B.
Lippincott & Co., 1877

In Old Plantation Days, Paul Laurence Dunbar,
Curtis Publishing Co., 1899

Slavery in the Cities of the South 1820-1860, Richard C. Wade, Oxford University Press, 1964

Red Over Black, Black Slavery Among the Cherokee Indians, R. Halliburton, Jr., Greenwood Press, 1968

100 Years of Lynchings, Ralph Ginzburg, Lancer Books, 1974

Slave Testimony, Edited by John W. Blassingame, Louisiana State University, 1975

Slave Culture, Sterling Stuckey, Oxford University Press, 1987

White over Blacks, 1550 to 1812, Winthrop D. Jordan, University of North Carolina, 1968

Red, White and Black, Gary B. Nash, Prentice Hall, Inc., 1974

Settlers on the Eastern Shore 1607 to 1750, John Anthony Scott, Alfred A. Knopf, 1967

The Slave Community, John W. Blassingame, Oxford University Press, 1972

Slavery Time When I Was Chillun Down on Marster's Plantation, Edited by Ronald Killion and Charles Waller, Beehive Press, 1973

Twelve Years A Slave, Sol Northrup, Louisiana State University Press, 1968

My Bondage and My Freedom, Frederick Douglass, Johnson Publishing Co., 1970

Incidents in the "Life of a Slave Girl," Harriet A. Jacobs, Harvard University Press, 1986

The Right of Search and The Slave Trade in Anglo-American Relations 1814-1862, Hugh G. Soulsby, Ph.D., The Johns Hopkins Press, 1933

Medicine and Slavery, Todd L. Savitt, The Board of Trustees of the University of Illinois, 1978

Manic Depressive Reactions in Negroes, Publications of the Association for Research in Nervous and Mental Disease, Manic-Depressive Psychosis, Nolan D.C. Lewis, and Louis D. Hubbard, 1931

American Negro Slavery, Ulrich Bonnell Phillips, Ph.D., D. Appleton-Century Company, 1936

The Slave Drivers, William L. Van Deburg, Greenwood Press Inc., 1979

Inside View of Slavery: or a Tour Among The Planters, C.G. Parsons, M.D., Argosy-Antiquarian Ltd., 1969

The Stranger in America 1793-1806, Charles William Janson, The Press Of The Pioneers Inc., 1935

The Slave Trade, Slavery and Color, Theodore D. Jervey, Metro Books Inc., 1972

Understanding Survivors of Abuse, Jane Levine Powers and Barbara Weiss Jaklitsch, Lexington Books, 1989

Life is Goodbye Life is Hello, Grieving Well Through All Kinds of Loss, Alla Bozarth-Campbell, Ph.D., CompCare Publishers, 1982

What Murder Leaves Behind, The Victim's Family, Doug Magee, Dodd, Mead and Company, 1983

Families in Peril, An Agenda For Social Change, Marian Wright Edelman, Harvard University Press, 1987

Adoption, A Handful of Hope, Suzanne Arms, Celestial Arts, 1990

Why Men Are The Way They Are, The Male-Female Dynamic, Warren Farrell, Ph.D., McGraw-Hill Book Company, 1986

Psycho-Cybernetics, Maxwell Maltz, M.D., Prentice-Hall, 1960

Think Black, An Introduction to Black Political Power, Frank McQuilkin, The Bruce Publishing Company, 1970

Black Women in White America, A Documentary History, Gerda Lerner, Vintage Books, 1973

Generation to Generation, Conversations on Religious Education and Culture, John H. Westerhoff III and Gwen Kennedy Neville, The Church Press, 1974

The Political Economy of the Black Ghetto, William K. Tabb, W.W. Norton and Company Inc., 1970

The Post-Industrial Utopians, Boris Frankel, The University of Wisconsin Press, 1987

Slavery and Race in American Popular Culture, William L. Van Deburg, The University of Wisconsin, 1984

Being Black: psychological-sociological dilemmas, Robert V. Guthrie, Canfield Press, 1970

On Being Negro in America, Saunders Redding, Bantam Books, 1951

Understanding Other People, Stuart Palmer, Fawcett Publications, 1966

Personal Politics, The Roots of Women's Liberation in the Civil Rights Movement and the New Left, Sara Evans, Vintage Books, 1979

An Uncharted Journey, Bertha C. Reynolds, NASW Press, 1963

Repressed Memories, Renee Fredrickson, Ph.D., Simon and Schuster, 1992

The Hare Plan, Nathan Hare, Ph.D., and Julia Hare, Ed.D., The Black Think Tank, 1991

Endless Enemies, Johnathan Kwitny, Penguin Books, 1984

God The Black Man and Truth, Ben Ammi,
Communicators Press, 1982

Curious Customs, Tad Tuleja, The Stonesong Press
Inc., 1987

The Confessions of Nat Turner, William Styron,
Bantam Books, 1966

The Crusade Against Slavery, Louis Filler, Harper
and Brothers, 1960

Black Power, Stokely Carmichael and Charles V.
Hamilton, Vintage Books, 1967

Racial Politics in American Cities, Rufus P. Browning,
Dale Rogers Marshall and David H. Tabb,
Longman Companies, 1990

Visions for Black Men, Na'im Akbar, Winston-Derek
Publishers Inc., 1991

100 Ways to Enhance Self-Concept in the Classroom,
Jack Canfield and Harold C. Wells, Prentice-Hall,
1976

The Great American History Fact-Finder, Ted Vanak and
Pam Cornelison, Houghton Mifflin Company, 1993

Middle Passage, Charles Johnson, Plume Books, 1991

*The Destruction of Western Civilization, as Seen
Through Islam, Christianity and Judaism*, Dr.
Khalid Abdullah Tariq Al-Mansour, The First
African Arabian Press, 1982

Experimental Psychology, Robert S. Woodworth and Harold Schlosberg, Holt, Rinehart and Winston, 1938

The Mark of Oppression, Abram Kardiner, M.D. and Lionel Ovesey, M.D., The World Publishing Company, 1962

Student Life and Customs, Henry D. Sheldon, Ph.D., D. Appleton and Company, 1901

Tribalism, Mysticism, Primitivism and The Rise of Genocide Against The African World, Batu A. Shakari, Shakari Publications, 1991

Dependence: A Sketch for a Portrait of the Dependent, Albert Memmi, Beacon Press, 1984

Hostage I: Kidnapping and Terrorism in our Time, L.B. Taylor, Jr., Franklin Watts, 1989

Bereavement, David A. Crenshaw, Continuum, 1990

Message To The Blackman in America, Elijah Muhammad, Muhammad's Temple No. 2, 1965

Black Gods of The Metropolis, Arthur Huff Fauset, University of Pennsylvania Press, 1944

Control Freaks, Gerald W. Piaget, Ph.D., Doubleday, 1991

The Adoption Life Cycle, Elinor B. Rosenberg, The Free Press, 1992

A *History of the South*, Francis Butler Simkins and Charles Pierce Roland, Alfred A. Knopf Inc., 1947

Being Adopted, David M. Brodzinsky, Ph.D., Marshall D. Schecter, M.D., Robin Marantz Henig, Anchor Books and Doubleday, 1992

Stump Speeches – Monologues . . . Conundrums . . . Etc., J. Melville Janson, David McKay Publisher, 1895

This book is further dedicated to a few of our deceased family who were murdered by the enemy:

Freddie Gray

Walter Scott

Tamir Rice

Eric Garner

Trayvon Martin

Jordan Davis

Michael Brown

Sean Bell

Akai Garley

Ramarley Graham

By the time this book is printed there will probably be more names to add to this list. We honor them all.